EURIPIDES · V

Electra
The Phoenician Women
The Bacchae

THE COMPLETE GREEK TRAGEDIES

Edited by David Grene and Richmond Lattimore

EURIPIDES · V

ELECTRA
Translated by Emily Townsend Vermeule

THE PHOENICIAN WOMEN
Translated by Elizabeth Wyckoff

THE BACCHAE
Translated by William Arrowsmith

Chronological Note on the Plays of Euripides
By Richmond Lattimore

THE UNIVERSITY OF CHICAGO PRESS

CHICAGO & LONDON

THE UNIVERSITY OF CHICAGO PRESS, CHICAGO 60637

The University of Chicago Press, Ltd., London

International Standard Book Number: 0-226-30784-0

Library of Congress Catalog Card Number: 55-5787

TABLE OF CONTENTS

ELECTRA

Translated by Emily Townsend Vermeule

INTRODUCTION TO *ELECTRA*

THE *Electra* was almost certainly produced in 413 B.C., between the sailing of the relief expedition to Sicily which the Dioscuri are rushing to protect (l. 1347) and the fleet's destruction in September. It thus falls squarely in Euripides' middle group of unorthodox Trojan War "tragedies" and contains elements of all their qualities: the bitter pathos of *Trojan Women* (415 B.C.), the romantic melodrama of *Iphigenia among the Taurians* (414 B.C.), the farce of *Helen* (412 B.C.). It also looks back to *Andromache* (419 B.C.) and forward to *Orestes* (408 B.C.) as a study in war-bred delinquency and is tempered by its own special quality as a tabloid thriller.

With this mixture of dramatic tones, *Electra* has received equally mixed critical notices, from Schlegel's "a singular monument of poetical, or rather unpoetical, perversity" to Murray's "close-knit, powerful . . . intellectual, rebellious." The play is undoubtedly perverse; it is also undoubtedly well constructed (better than *Choephoroe* or Sophocles' *Electra*). It is fast-paced, logical, exciting. The main offense is in the characters, and, secondarily, the choral *embolima*, which generally seem irrelevant, the careless repetition of words, the falling out of character in long speeches, and the lack of poetic grandeur.

At first reading, many points of style and content seem so deliberately in bad taste that one suspects an entire parody of tragedy in the high style, apart from the mockery of *Choephoroe* in the tokens scene. To the unsympathetic it can seem enormously funny, and prohibitive to tragic response, when Aegisthus is nervous that Electra may have a baby even if kept under lock and key, when she makes her tragic entrance with a water pot, when Orestes asks if the Farmer finds her too unattractive to sleep with, when Electra sends Orestes off to death and slaughter like Mabel in *The Pirates of Penzance*, when she complains that no one likes her well enough to be her midwife (which is not surprising if she washes as little as she says). Yet all this grows out of Euripides' chosen characterization of Electra, based firmly on Sophocles' conception of that model heroine: unwashed, in rags, a slave princess, longing for attention and some emotional outlet, morbidly attached to her dead father, powerfully jealous of Clytemnestra, vindictive and efficient.

Euripides adds new insights, mainly Electra's failure to distinguish right from wrong; her daydreams limited to clothes, marriage, money; her subtle streak of nymphomania. But, while exposing her psychology with a ruthless scalpel and pushing Sophocles' character to its logical extreme, he has lost sight of the spiritual strength with which Sophocles endowed her, and so sacrifices that sympathy for the protagonist which is essential to tragedy. Again from Sophocles, Orestes takes on some of Chrysothemis' ethos, as a foil to Electra, with the added spice of having to pay for her decisions while she goes free. The Pedagogue has split into Euripides' Farmer and Old Man, the former full of rustic aphorisms and kindness, the latter again strategic co-ordinator for his emotional charges. Clytemnestra owes something to Sophocles' portrayal of middle-class grandeur, but with less imagination and authority, more vanity and torment. Aegisthus we see from two angles: in Electra's prejudiced testimony, as a drunken bully and seducer; in the Messenger's account of his death, as an affable and pious host. Indeed this double vision is true of the whole play, as Electra's image of the truth, and the truth itself, stubbornly refuse to match.

The astigmatism is deliberate. While inspired by Sophocles' power of characterization, Euripides apparently disapproves of his freeing the protagonists from the painful aftereffects of murder and so reverts to Aeschylus in matters like the blood-curse, the Furies, and the trial, recapitulating *Eumenides* in his Epilogue. But Aeschylean morality is somehow missing, and by the end of the play we see that Euripides has been playing falsely with both his sources, and, by jamming the characters of Sophocles into the framework of Aeschylus, has destroyed the validity of both. There emerges a true Euripidean demonstration that life resists formula and that even a moral situation as clear as the one confronting the heirs of Agamemnon is chaotic when seen from the inside.

The abstract moral justification for murdering Clytemnestra and Aegisthus is the same as earlier; it is even more cogent here, with a blood-price set on Orestes' head, new children to usurp the dynasty,

Electra's forced marriage to a peasant. But the strength of the moral position depends on the characters involved. When the protagonists are as unsympathetic as here, when the victims are hit from behind at a sacrifice or ambushed in the role of compassionate grandmother, must we shift our moral judgments or acknowledge the justice of the murders while admitting that we personally find them a little hard to take? If Hadas feels that "Electra is a self-pitying slattern, Orestes a timid ruffian, Clytemnestra a suburban clubwoman, Aegisthus a courteous and popular ruler, the murders as dastardly as conceivable," or Rose calls Orestes and Electra "fanatical monomaniacs," they have fallen into Euripides' trap. He is challenging the audience to maintain moral clarity in the face of extreme distaste for the agents of justice, who do irreparable damage out of confused and flippant motives with the guidance of heaven. *Electra* is another phase in his campaign against Apollo, the morality of the gods, and tender-minded human champions of "justice"—a concept in fact cold and difficult, admirable in the abstract, ugly in concrete situations.

The double vision of character is Euripides' demonstration tool, a technique of seducing the audience into sympathy with the protagonists and then destroying that sympathy by a display of wanton brutality. This is familiar from *Medea*, *Hecuba*, *Heracles*, *Bacchae*. The play begins along orthodox melodramatic lines: injured innocents, lost birthright and love, cruel usurpers, the dead calling for vengeance. But gradually we realize that neither Electra nor Orestes is capable of serious thought. Orestes relies on Apollo's oracle until actually faced with his mother and a knife; when he tries to withdraw in emotional chaos, Electra drives him on. She has no oracle, only a lust for revenge. Both children are more concerned with their standard of living than with morality; their lost ancestral home looms largest in their minds as a paradise of rugs, good food, money; to Electra the fact that Clytemnestra saved her from death at Aegisthus' hands means less than the clothes of the Trojan slaves. Electra never realizes, Orestes only dimly, that they are committing exactly the same atrocity for which they want to punish their elders. With the confused thinking characteristic of obsessive neurotics, they believe that killing their mother will somehow make her love them again, so that they can settle down and be happy. Their surprise at the results is more disturbing than their pain.

Orestes scarcely mentions his father. Electra has a genuine attachment to him, which Clytemnestra notes she showed as a child and which has doubtless grown stronger since his death. But when she comes to condemn Clytemnestra, her tirade is almost entirely in terms of her mother's sexual escapades and femininity, which Electra envies while refusing to imitate. Jealousy of her mother rather than love for her father drives her on, so that we hear a good deal about Clytemnestra's looks and clothes and her two marriages, while Electra's fiancé was unfairly translated to godhead, her other suitors turned from the door, and her present husband scarcely what she wishes in terms of breeding, money, or marital affection. The content of her nocturnal brooding is clear from the way she taunts dead Aegisthus with his looks and adulteries and refuses to have him as a husband. This is objectively irrelevant, since he had other interests and is dead, but psychologically revealing, for she must have watched him closely during her period of forcibly extended virginity. Orestes' suggestion that Aegisthus expects another child (l. 626) puts the false-baby notion in her mind, an unconscious perfect choice of bait for Clytemnestra. Her fear of Orestes' touch, her insistence to complete strangers on her married virginity, her first reaction to the murder: Who will marry me now?—all underline the frustration implicit in her name.

The characterization may be ugly, but it is brilliant and convincing. It is deliberately calculated to alienate us from "the right side"; Electra's initial suffering explains but does not excuse her subsequent viciousness. The victims have been alienated by their cruelty, vanity, and sordid private lives, which their flickering kindness does not sufficiently relieve. Apollo is alienated by a label of brutal ignorance. There is no focus of sympathy left, only a pervasive bad taste which leads to disgust with all forms of violence.

The question is whether Euripides enjoyed the psychological exploration of suffering for its own sake, or had a moral purpose. In the first case, one tags the play with *pathei pathos* or "suffering brutalizes," and shelves it as a work of uncomfortable insight. In the second case one is forced to consider Euripides' theme that good and evil bear no relation to human character, are beyond the reach of simple formula, possibly do not exist at all. In either case *Electra* cannot be dismissed as wilful or perverse. It is a planned demonstration that personal relationships, human or divine, are inescapably fraught with indecency and that justice can be as ugly as crime.

The text followed is J. D. Denniston's Oxford edition (1939), based on Murray. I have omitted lines 899 and 1097–1101 (= fragment 464, *Cretan Women*) and changed the order of speakers at 677–81 to accord with Denniston's tentative suggestion.

ELECTRA

CHARACTERS

Farmer, a Mycenaean

Electra

Orestes

Pylades, a mute character

Chorus of Argive peasant women

Old Man

Messenger

Clytemnestra

Dioscuri: Castor, and Polydeuces, a mute character

ELECTRA

SCENE: *A high bare slope of the Argive hills commanding a view of the*
road to Argos, stage left, and the southern passes toward Sparta,
right. A square timber-and-mudbrick cottage stands in the center.
The time is the end of night with stars still in the sky. The Farmer
stands looking down toward the river valley and the sea.

Farmer

Argos, old bright floor of the world, Inachus' pouring
tides—King Agamemnon once on a thousand ships
hoisted the war god here and sailed across to Troy.
He killed the monarch of the land of Ilium,
Priam; he sacked the glorious city of Dardanus;   5
he came home safe to Argos and high on the towering shrines
nailed up the massive loot of Barbary for the gods.
So, over there he did well. But in his own house
he died in ambush planned for him by his own wife
Clytemnestra and by her lover Aegisthus' hand.   10
    He lost the ancient scepter of Tantalus; he is dead.
Thyestes' son Aegisthus walks king in the land
and keeps the dead man's wife for himself, Tyndareus' child.
As for the children he left home when he sailed to Troy,
his son Orestes and his flowering girl Electra,   15
Orestes almost died under Aegisthus' fist,
but his father's ancient servant snatched the boy away,
gave him to Strophius to bring up in the land of Phocis.
Electra waited motionless in her father's house.
But when the burning season of young ripeness took her,   20
then the great princes of the land of Greece came begging
her bridal. Aegisthus was afraid. Afraid her son
if noble in blood would punish Agamemnon's death.
He held her in the house sundered from every love.
Yet, even guarded so, she filled his nights with fear   25
lest she in secret to some prince might still bear sons;

he laid his plans to kill her. But her mother, though
savage in soul, then saved her from Aegisthus' blow.
The lady found excuse for murdering her husband
but flinched from killing a child, afraid of the world's contempt.   30
Later Aegisthus framed a new design. He swore
to any man who captured Agamemnon's son
running in exile and murdered him, a price of gold.
Electra—he gave her to me as a gift, to hold
her as my wife.

        Now, I was born of Mycenaean   35
family, on this ground I have nothing to be ashamed of,
in breeding they shone bright enough. But in their fortune
they ranked as paupers, which blots out all decent blood.
He gave her to me, a weak man, to weaken his own fear,
for if a man of high position had taken her   40
he might have roused awake the sleeping Agamemnon's
blood—justice might have knocked at Aegisthus' door.
I have not touched her and the love-god Cypris knows it:
I never shamed the girl in bed, she is still virgin.
I would feel ugly holding down the gentle daughter   45
of a king in violence, I was not bred to such an honor.
And poor laboring Orestes whom they call my brother—
I suffer his grief, I think his thoughts, if he came home
to Argos and saw his sister so doomed in her wedding.

    Whoever says that I am a born fool to keep   50
a young girl in my house and never touch her body,
or says I measure wisdom by a crooked line
of morals, should know he is as great a fool as I.

                (*Electra enters from the cottage carrying a water jar on
                          her head and talking to herself.*)

Electra

    O night, black night, whose breast nurses the golden stars,
I wander through your darkness, head lifted to bear   55
this pot I carry to the sources of the river—
I am not forced, I chose this slavery myself

to illuminate Aegisthus' arrogance for the gods—
and cry my pain to Father in the great bright air.
For my own mother, she, Tyndareus' deadly daughter,   60
has thrown me out like dirt from the house, to her husband's joy,
and while she breeds new children in Aegisthus' bed
has made me and Orestes aliens to her love.

Farmer

Now why, unhappy girl, must you for my sake wrestle
such heavy work though you were raised in luxury?   65
Each time I mention it you flash into rebellion.

Electra

I think you equal to the gods in kindliness,
for you have never hurt me though I am in trouble.
It is great fortune for men to find a kind physician
of suffering, which I have found in finding you.   70
Indeed without your bidding I should make the labor
as light as I have strength for; you will bear it better
if I claim some share with you in the work. Outdoors
you have enough to do; my place is in the house,
to keep it tidy. When a man comes in from work   75
it is sweet to find his hearthplace looking swept and clean.

Farmer

Well, if your heart is set on helping, go. The spring
is not so distant from the house. At light of dawn
I will put the cows to pasture and start planting the fields.
A lazy man may rustle gods upon his tongue   80
but never makes a living if he will not work.

> (*They go off together, stage right. Enter Orestes and Pylades
> from the mountain road, quickly but cautiously, and as-
> sure themselves the coast is clear.*)

Orestes

Pylades, I consider you the first of men
in loyalty and love to me, my host and friend.

You only of my friends gave honor and respect
to Orestes, suffering as I suffer from Aegisthus.   85
He killed my father—he and my destructive mother.
I come from secret converse with the holy god
to this outpost of Argos—no one knows I am here—
to counterchange my father's death for death to his killers.
During the night just passed I found my father's tomb,   90
gave him my tears in gift and sheared my hair in mourning
and sprinkled ceremonial sheep's blood on the fire,
holding the rite concealed from the tyrants who rule here.

    I will not set my foot inside the city walls.
I chose this gatepost of the land deliberately,   95
compacting a double purpose. First, if any spy
should recognize me I can run for foreign soil,
second, to find my sister. For they say she married
and, tamed to domestic love, lives here no longer virgin.
I want to be with her and take her as my partner   100
in the work and learn precise news from behind the walls.

    And now, since lady dawn is lifting her white face,
smooth out our footprints from the path and come away.
Perhaps a field-bound farmer or some cottage wife
will meet us on the road, and we can ask discreetly   105
whether my sister lives anywhere in these hills.

    Quick now! I see some sort of serving girl approach
with a jar of fountain water on her shaven head—
it looks heavy for her. Sit down here, let us question
the slave girl. Pylades, perhaps at last we shall hear   110
the news we hoped for when we crossed into this land.

*(They hide behind the altar in front of the cottage. Electra
comes back along the path with her jar, singing
aloud, half dancing.)*

Electra

    Quicken the foot's rush—time has struck—O
walk now, walk now weeping aloud,
      O for my grief!

I was bred Agamemnon's child,   115
formed in the flesh of Clytemnestra
    Tyndareus' hellish daughter,
Argos' people have named me true:
        wretched Electra.
Cry, cry for my labor and pain,   120
    cry for the hatred of living.
Father who in the halls of death
lie hacked by your wife and Aegisthus, O
    help, Agamemnon!

Come, waken the mourning again,   125
bring me again the sweetness of tears.

Quicken the foot's rush—time has struck—
walk now, walk now weeping aloud,
    O for my grief!
In what city and in what house, O   130
brother of grief, do you walk a slave?
    You left me locked in the cursed
palace chambers for doom to strike
        your sister in sorrow.
Come, loose me from labor, come   135
    save me in pity, O Zeus,
Zeus, for our father's hate-spilled blood
help storm the wicked and harbor our lost
        voyager in Argos.

Set this vessel down from my head, O   140
take it, while I lift music of mourning
        by night to my father.
Father, the maenad song of death
    I cry you among the dead
beneath the earth, the words I pour   145
    day after day unending
as I move, ripping my flesh with sharp

nails, fists pounding my clipped
    head for your dying.

Ai, ai, tear my face!   150
I, like the swan of echoing song
in descant note at the water's edge
who calls to its parent so dearly loved
and dying now in the hidden net
of twisted meshes, mourn you thus   155
    in agony dying,

body steeped in the final bath,
lull most pitiful, sleep of death.
    O for my grief!
Bitter the ax and bitter the gash,   160
  bitter the road you walked
from Troy straight to their plotted net—
    your lady did not receive you
with victor's ribbons or flowers to crown you,
but with double-edged steel she made you
savage sport for Aegisthus, gave you   165
    to her shifty lover.

            (*The chorus of Argive peasant women enters from the*
                 Mycenae road to confront Electra.)

Chorus
    Princess, daughter of Agamemnon,
we have come to your country court,
      Electra, to see you.
There passed, passed me a man
      bred on the milk of the hills,
a Mycenaean mountaineer   170
who gave me word that on the third
day the Argives herald abroad
a holy feast, when all the girls
will pass in procession up to the temple of Hera.

Electra

    Dear friends, not for shimmering robes,   175
not for twisted bracelets of gold
    does my heart take wing in delight.
I am too sad, I cannot stand
    in choral joy with the maidens
or beat the tune with my whirling foot;   180
    rather with tears by night
and tears by day shall I fill my soul
    shaking in grief and fear.
Look! think! would my filthy locks
and robe all torn into slavish rags   185
do public honor to Agamemnon's
    daughter, the princess?
honor to Troy which will never forget
    my conquering father?

Chorus

    Great, great is the goddess. Come,   190
I will lend you a dress to wear,
    thick-woven of wool,
and gold—be gracious, accept—
                  gold for holiday glitter.
Do you think your tears and holding back
honor from god will ever hurt   195
your haters? Not by sounding lament
but only by prayer and reverent love
for the gods, my child, will you learn to live gentler days.

Electra

    Gods? Not one god has heard
my helpless cry or watched of old   200
    over my murdered father.
Mourn again for the wasted dead,
    mourn for the living outlaw

somewhere prisoned in foreign lands
    moving through empty days,
passing from one slave hearth to the next   205
    though born of a glorious sire.
And I! I in a peasant's hut
waste my life like wax in the sun,
thrust and barred from my father's home
    to a scarred mountain exile   210
while my mother rolls in her bloody bed
    and plays at love with a stranger.

Chorus

    Like Helen, your mother's sister—Helen charged and found
    guilty of massive pain to Greece and all your house.

Electra

    Oh, oh! women, I break from my deathbound cry.   215
    Look! there are strangers here close to the house who crouch
    huddled beside the altar and rise up in ambush.
    Run, you take the path and I into the house
    with one swift rush can still escape these criminals.

Orestes

    Poor girl, stand still, and fear not. I would never hurt you.   220

Electra

    Phoebus Apollo, help! I kneel to you. Do not kill me.

Orestes

    I hope I shall kill others hated more than you.

Electra

    Get out; don't touch. You have no right to touch my body.

Orestes

    There is no person I could touch with greater right.

Electra

    Why were you hiding, sword in hand, so near my house?   225

Orestes

    Stand still and listen. You will agree I have rights here.

Electra

    I stand here utterly in your power. You are stronger.

Orestes

    I have come to bring you a spoken message from your brother.

Electra

    Dearest of strangers, is he alive or is he dead?

Orestes

    Alive. I wish to give you all the best news first.   230

Electra

    God bless your days, as you deserve for such sweet words.

Orestes

    I share your gift with you that we may both be blessed.

Electra

    Where is he now, attempting to bear unbearable exile?

Orestes

    He is wrecked, nor can conform to any city's code.

Electra

    Tell me, he is not poor? not hungry for daily bread?   235

Orestes

    He has bread, yet he has the exile's constant hunger.

Electra

    You came to bring a message—what are his words for me?

Orestes

"Are you alive? Where are you living? What is your life?"

Electra

I think you see me. First, my body wasted and dry—

Orestes

Sadness has wasted you so greatly I could weep.   240

Electra

Next, my head razor-cropped like a victim of the Scythians.

Orestes

Your brother's life and father's death both bite at your heart.

Electra

Alas, what else have I? I have no other loves.

Orestes

You grieve me. Whom do you think your brother loves but you?

Electra

He is not here. He loves me, but he is not here.   245

Orestes

Why do you live in a place like this, so far from town?

Electra

Because I married, stranger—a wedding much like death.

Orestes

Bad news for your brother. Your husband is a Mycenaean?

Electra

But not the man my father would have wished me to marry.

Orestes

Tell me. I am listening, I can speak to your brother.   250

Electra

This is his house. I live quite isolated here.

Orestes

A ditch-digger, a cowherd would look well living here.

Electra

He is a poor man but well born, and he respects me.

Orestes

Respects? What does your husband understand by "respect"?

Electra

He has never been violent or touched me in my bed.   255

Orestes

A vow of chastity? or he finds you unattractive?

Electra

He finds it attractive not to insult my royal blood.

Orestes

How could he not be pleased at marrying so well?

Electra

He judges the man who gave me had no right to, stranger.

Orestes

I see—afraid Orestes might avenge your honor.   260

Electra

Afraid of that, yes—he is also decent by nature.

Orestes

Ah.
You paint one of nature's gentlemen. We must pay him well.

Electra

We will, if my absent brother ever gets home again.

Orestes

Your mother took the wedding calmly, I suppose?

Electra

Women save all their love for lovers, not for children.   265

Orestes

What was in Aegisthus' mind, to insult you so?

Electra

He hoped that I, so wedded, would have worthless sons.

Orestes

Too weak for undertaking blood-revenge on him?

Electra

That was his hope. I hope to make him pay for it.

Orestes

This husband of your mother's—does he know you are virgin?   270

Electra

No, he knows nothing. We have played our parts in silence.

Orestes

These women listening as we talk are friends of yours?

Electra

Good enough friends to keep our words kindly concealed.

Orestes

How should Orestes play *his* part, if he comes to Argos?

Electra

If he comes? ugly talk. The time has long been ripe.   275

Orestes

Say he comes, still how could he kill his father's killers?

Electra

As Father suffered let our enemies suffer too.

Orestes

Mother and lover both? are you bold for that killing?

Electra

Mother by the same ax that cut Father to ruin.

Orestes

May I tell him what you say and how determined you are? 280

Electra

Tell him how gladly I would die in Mother's blood.

Orestes

O, I wish Orestes could stand here and listen.

Electra

Yet if I saw him I should hardly know him, sir.

Orestes

No wonder. You were both very young when you were parted.

Electra

I have only one friend who might still know his face. 285

Orestes

The man who saved him once from death, as the story goes?

Electra

Yes, old now and old even when he nursed my father.

Orestes

When your father died did his body find some burial?

Electra

He found what he found. He was thrown on the dirt outdoors.

Orestes

    I cannot bear it. What have you said? Even a stranger's   290
    pain bites strangely deep and hurts us when we hear it.
    Tell me the rest, and with new knowledge I will bring
    Orestes your tale, so harsh to hear and so compelling
    when heard. Uneducated men are pitiless,
    but we who are educated pity much. And we pay   295
    a high price for being intelligent. Wisdom hurts.

Chorus

    The same excitement stirs my mind in this as yours—
    I live far from the city and I know its troubles
    hardly at all. Now I would like to learn them too.

Electra

    I will tell if I must—and must tell you who love me—   300
    how my luck, and my father's, is too heavy to lift.
    Since you have moved me to speak so, stranger, I must beg
    that you will tell Orestes all my distress, and his.
    First tell him how I am kept like a beast in stable rags,
    my skin heavy with grease and dirt. Describe to him   305
    this hut—*my* home, who used to live in the king's palace.
    I weave my clothes myself and slavelike at the loom
    must work or else walk naked through the world in nothing.
    I fetch and carry water from the riverside,
    I am deprived of holy festivals and dances,   310
    I cannot talk to women since I am a girl,
    I cannot think of Castor, who was close in blood
    and loved me once, before he rose among the gods.
    My mother in the glory of her Phrygian rugs
    sits on the throne, while circled at her feet the girls   315
    of Asia stoop, whom Father won at the sack of Troy,
    their clothes woven in snowy wool from Ida, pinned
    with golden brooches, while the walls and floor are stained
    still with my father's black and rotting blood. The man
    who murdered him goes riding grand in Father's chariot,   320

with bloody hands and high delight lifting the staff
of office by which Father marshaled the Greek lords.
The tomb of Agamemnon finds no honor yet,
never yet drenched with holy liquids or made green
in myrtle branches, barren of bright sacrifice.   325
But in his drunken fits, my mother's lover, brilliant
man, triumphant leaps and dances on the mound
or pelts my father's stone memorial with rocks
and dares to shout against us with his boldened tongue:
"Where is your son Orestes? When will that noble youth   330
come to protect your tomb?" Insults to empty space.
    Kind stranger, as I ask you, tell him all these things.
For many call him home again—I speak for them—
the voices in our hands and tongues and grieving minds
and heads, shaven in mourning; and his father calls.   335
All will be shamed if he whose father captured Troy
cannot in single courage kill a single man,
although his strength is younger and his blood more noble.

Chorus

Electra! I can see your husband on the road.
He has finished his field work and is coming home.   340

> (*The Farmer enters from the left to con-
> front the group by his house.*)

Farmer

Hey there! who are these strangers standing at our gates?
What is the errand that could bring them to our rough
courtyard? Are they demanding something from me? A nice
woman should never stand in gossip with young men.

Electra

My dearest husband, do not come suspecting me.   345
You shall hear their story, the whole truth. They come
as heralds to me with new tidings of Orestes.
Strangers, I ask you to forgive him what he said.

Farmer

What news? Is Orestes still alive in the bright light?

Electra

So they have told me, and I do not doubt their words.   350

Farmer

Does he still remember his father, and your troubles?

Electra

We hope so. But an exile is a helpless man.

Farmer

Then what are these plans of his? What have they come to tell?

Electra

He sent them simply to see my troubles for themselves.

Farmer

What they don't see themselves I imagine you have told them.   355

Electra

They know it all. I took good care that they missed nothing.

Farmer

Why were our doors not opened to them long ago?
Move into the house, you will find entertainment
to answer your good news, such as my roof can offer.
Servants, pick up their baggage, bring their spears indoors.   360
Come, no polite refusals. You are here as friends
most dear to me who meet you now. Though I am poor
in money, I think you will not find our manners poor.

Orestes

By the gods! is this the man who helps you keep your marriage
a fiction, who has no desire to shame Orestes?   365

Electra

This is the man they know as poor Electra's husband.

Orestes

Alas,
we look for good on earth and cannot recognize it
when met, since all our human heritage runs mongrel.
At times I have seen descendants of the noblest family
grow worthless though the cowards had courageous sons;   370
inside the souls of wealthy men bleak famine lives
while minds of stature struggle trapped in starving bodies.

How then can man distinguish man, what test can he use?
the test of wealth? that measure means poverty of mind;
of poverty? the pauper owns one thing, the sickness   375
of his condition, a compelling teacher of evil;
by nerve in war? yet who, when a spear is cast across
his face, will stand to witness his companion's courage?
We can only toss our judgments random on the wind.

This fellow here is no great man among the Argives,   380
not dignified by family in the eyes of the world—
he is a face in the crowd, and yet we choose him champion.
Can you not come to understand, you empty-minded,
opinion-stuffed people, a man is judged by grace
among his fellows, manners are nobility's touchstone?   385
Such men of manners can control our cities best,
and homes, but the well-born sportsman, long on muscle, short
on brains, is only good for a statue in the park,
not even sterner in the shocks of war than weaker
men, for courage is the gift of character.   390
Now let us take whatever rest this house can give;
Agamemnon's child deserves it, the one here and the one
absent for whom I stand. We have no choice but go
indoors, servants, inside the house, since our poor host
seems eager to entertain us, more than a rich man might.   395
I do praise and admire his most kind reception
but would have been more pleased if your brother on the crest

of fortune could have brought me to a more fortunate house.
Perhaps he may still come; Apollo's oracles
are strong, though human prophecy is best ignored.   400

(*Orestes and Pylades go into the house.*)

Chorus

Now more than ever in our lives, Electra, joy
makes our hearts light and warm. Perhaps your fortune, first
running these painful steps, will stride to the goal in glory.

Electra

You are thoughtless. You know quite well the house is bare;
why take these strangers in? They are better born than you.   405

Farmer

Why? Because if they are the gentlemen they seem,
will they not treat the small as gently as the great?

Electra

Small is the word for you. Now the mistake is made,
go quickly to my father's loved and ancient servant
who by Tanaos' river, where it cuts the hills   410
of Argos off from Spartan country, goes his rounds
watching his flocks in distant exile from the town.
Tell him these strangers have descended on me; ask
him to come and bring some food fit for distinguished guests.
He will surely be happy; he will bless the gods   415
when he hears the child he saved so long ago still lives.
Besides, we cannot get any help from Father's house,
from Mother—our news would fly to her on bitter wings,
bold though she is, if she should hear Orestes lives.

Farmer

Well, if you wish it, I can pass your message on   420
to the old man. But you get quick into the house
and ready up what's there. A woman when she has to
can always find some food to set a decent table.

(*Electra goes into the cottage.*)

The house holds little, yet it is enough, I know,
to keep these strangers choked with food at least one day.   425
    In times like these, when wishes soar but power fails,
I contemplate the steady comfort found in gold:
gold you can spend on guests; gold you can pay the doctor
when you get sick. But a small crumb of gold will buy
our daily bread, and when a man has eaten that,   430
you cannot really tell the rich and poor apart.

(*The farmer goes off right, toward the hills.*)

Chorus

O glorious ships who sailed across to Troy once
    moving on infinite wooden oars
guarding the circling choir of Nereid dancers
where the dolphin shook in love at the flute-   435
    melody and about the sea-
    blue prows went plunging
as he led the goddess Thetis' son,
light-striding Achilles, on his way
with Agamemnon to Ilium's cliffs   440
    where Simois pours in the sea.

Of old the Nereids passed Euboea's headlands
    bringing the heavy shield of gold,
forged on Hephaestus' anvil, and golden armor.
Up Mount Pelion, up the jut   445
    of Ossa's holy slopes on high,
    up the nymphs' spy-rocks
they hunted the aged horseman's hill
where he trained the boy as a dawn for Greece,
the son of Thetis, sea-bred and swift-   450
    lived in the Atreid wars.

Once I heard from a Trojan captive known to the port
    in Nauplia close to Argos
    of your brilliant shield, O goddess'
child, how in its circled space   455

these signs, scenes, were in blazon warning,
    mourning, for Phrygia:
running in frieze on its massive rim,
Perseus lifting the severed head
cut at the neck—with Gorgon beauty   460
he walks on wings over the sea;
Hermes is with him, angel of Zeus,
    great Maia's
child of the flocks and forests.

Out of the shield's curved center glittered afar the high
    shining round of the sun   465
    driving with wingèd horses,
and the chorused stars of upper air—
Pleiads, Hyads—Hector eyed them,
    swerving aside.
Over the helmet of beaten gold   470
Sphinxes snatch in hooking nails
their prey trapped with song. On the hollow
greave, the lioness' fire breath
flares in her clawed track as she runs,
    staring back
at the wind-borne foal of Peirene.   475

All along the blade of the deadly sword, hooves pounding,
horses leap; black above their backs the dust blows.
    Still this prince of arms and men
    you killed by lust of sex and sin   480
    of mind, Tyndarid Helen.
For this the sons of heaven will send
you yet among the dead; some far
day I shall still see your blood fall   485
red from your neck on the iron sword.

          (Enter the Old Man, alone, from the right,
                out of breath after climbing.)

Old Man

Where is my young mistress and my lady queen,
the child of Agamemnon, whom I raised and loved?
How steep this house seems set to me, with rough approach,
as I grow old for climbing on this withered leg.   490
But when your friends call, you must come and drag along
and hump your spine till it snaps and bend your knees like pins.

(*Electra enters from the cottage.*)

Why there she is—my daughter, look at you by the door!
I am here. I have brought you from my cropping sheep
a newborn lamb, a tender one, just pulled from the teat,   495
and flowers looped in garlands, cheese white from the churn,
and this stored treasure of the wine god, aged and spiked
with a pungent smell—not much of it, but sweet, and good
to pour into the cup with other weaker wine.
Let someone carry all this gear to the guests indoors,   500
for I have cried a little and would like to dry
my face and eyes out here on my cloak—more holes than wool.

Electra

Old uncle, father, why is your face so stained with tears?
After so long has my grief stirred your thoughts again,
or is it poor Orestes in his running days   505
you mourn for, or my father, whom your two old hands
once nursed and helped without reward for self or love?

Old Man

Reward, no. Yet I could not stop myself, in this:
for I came past his tomb and circled from the road
and fell to the earth there, weeping for its loneliness,   510
and let it drink, tapping this winesack for your guests
in brief libation, and I wreathed the stone in myrtle.
And there I saw on the burning-altar a black-fleeced
sheep, throat cut and blood still warm in its dark stream,
and curling locks of bright brown hair cut off in gift.   515

I stopped, quiet, to wonder, child, what man had courage
to visit at that tomb. It could not be an Argive.
Is there a chance your brother has arrived in secret
and paused to stare upon his father's shabby tomb?
Look at the lock of hair, match it to your own head,   520
see if it is not twin to yours in color and cut.
Often a father's blood, running in separate veins,
makes the two bodies almost mirrors in their form.

Electra

Old man, I always thought you were wiser than you sound
if you really think my brother, who is bright and bold,   525
would come to our land in hiding, frightened by Aegisthus.
Besides, how could a lock of his hair match with mine?
one from a man with rugged training in the ring
and games, one combed and girlish? It is not possible.
You may find many matching birds of the same feather   530
not bred in the same nest, old man, nor matched in blood.

Old Man

At least go set your foot in the print of his hunting boot
and see if it is not the same as yours, my child.

Electra

You make me angry. How could rocky ground receive
the imprint of a foot? And if it could be traced,   535
it would not be the same for brother and for sister,
a man's foot and a girl's—of course his would be bigger.

Old Man

Is there no sign then, if your brother should come home...
of loom or pattern by which you would know the cloth
you wove, I wrapped him in, to rescue him from death?   540

Electra

You know quite well Orestes went away in exile
when I was very small. If a little girl's hand

could weave, how could a growing boy still wear that cloth
unless his shirt and tunic lengthened with his legs?

    Some pitying stranger must have passed the tomb and cut   545
a mourning-lock, or townsmen slipping past the spies. . . .

Old Man

Where are the strangers now? I want to look them over
and draw them out with conversation of your brother.

        (Orestes and Pylades enter from the cottage.)

Electra

Here they come striding lightly from the cottage now.

Old Man

Well. They look highborn enough, but the coin may prove   550
false. Often a noble face hides filthy ways.
Nevertheless—
        Greetings, strangers, I wish you well.

Orestes

And greetings in return, old sir.
                Electra, where,
to what friends of yours, does this human antique belong?

Electra

This is the man who nursed and loved my father, sir.   555

Orestes

What! the one who saved your brother once from death?

Electra

Indeed he saved him—if indeed he still is safe.

Orestes

Ah, so!
Why do you stare upon me like a man who squints
at the bright stamp of a coin? Do I stir your memory?

Electra

Perhaps just happy seeing Orestes' twin in age.   560

Orestes

Dear Orestes. Why does he walk round me in circles?

Electra

Stranger, I am astonished too as I look at him.

Old Man

Mistress, now pray. Daughter Electra, pray to the gods.

Electra

For what of the things I have, or all I never had?

Old Man

For a treasure of love within your grasp, which god reveals.   565

Electra

As you please; I will pray the gods. What was in your mind?

Old Man

Look now upon this man, my child—your dearest love.

Electra

I have been looking rather at you; is your mind disturbed?

Old Man

My mind not steady when my eyes have seen your brother?

Electra

What have you said, old man? what hopeless impossible word?   570

Old Man

I said I see Orestes—here—Agamemnon's son.

Electra

How? What sign do you see? What can I know and trust?

Old Man

The scar above his eye where once he slipped and drew
blood as he helped you chase a fawn in your father's court.

Electra

I see the mark of a fall, but—I cannot believe—   575

Old Man

How long will you stand, hold yourself back from his arms and
    love?

Electra

I will not any longer, for my heart has trust
in the token you show.
                        O Brother so delayed by time,
I hold you against hope—

Orestes

                        Time hid you long from me.

Electra

I never promised myself—

Orestes

                        I had abandoned hope.   580

Electra

And are you he?

Orestes

                        I am, your sole defender and friend.
Now if I catch the prey for which I cast my net—

Electra

I trust you and trust in you. Never believe in god
again if evil can still triumph over good.

Chorus

You have come, you have come, our slow, bright day,   585
    you have shone, you have shown a beacon—

« 33 »

lit hope for the state, who fled of old
your father's palace, doomed and pained,
    drifting in exile.

Now god, some god restores us strong   590
    to triumph, my love.
Lift high your hands, lift high your voice, raise
prayers to the gods. In fortune, fortune
your brother shall march straight to the city's heart.   595

Orestes

Enough. I find sweet pleasure in embrace and welcome,
but let us give ourselves over to pleasure later.
Old man, you came on the crest of opportunity—
tell me what I must do to punish the murderer
and purify my mother from adultery.   600
Have I in Argos any strong measure of friends
or am I bankrupt in backing as I am in fortune?
Whom shall I look to? Shall it be by day or night?
What hunting-track will lead me toward my enemies?

Old Man

My son, you lost your friends when luck deserted you.   605
That would indeed be luck met on the road for you,
someone to share both good and evil without change.
But you from root to leaf-top have been robbed of friends
who, leaving, left you no bequest of hope. Hear me:
in your own hand and the grace of god you hold all poised   610
to capture back your city, place, and patrimony.

Orestes

But what should we be doing now to strike our target?

Old Man

Kill him. Kill Thyestes' son. And kill your mother.

Orestes

Such the triumphal crown I came for, yet—how reach it?

Old Man

Not inside the city even if you were willing.   615

Orestes

Is he so strongly fenced by bodyguards and spears?

Old Man

You know it. The man's afraid of you and cannot sleep.

Orestes

Let that go, then. Tell me another way, old man.

Old Man

Yes—you shall hear, for something came to me just now.

Orestes

I hope your plan and my reaction are equally good.   620

Old Man

I saw Aegisthus as I hauled my way up here.

Orestes

Good, that sounds hopeful. Where am I to find him now?

Old Man

Close, down in the meadows where his horses graze.

Orestes

What is he doing? Out of despair I see new light.

Old Man

Offering a banquet to the goddess Nymphs, I think.   625

Orestes

To keep his children safe? For a child soon to be born?

Old Man

I know only that he is prepared to kill a bull.

Orestes

How many men are with him? simply alone with servants?

Old Man

No citizens were there; a handful of palace servants.

Orestes

No one who might still recognize my face, old man?　　　　630

Old Man

They are his private servants and have never seen you.

Orestes

And would they, if we conquered, be, ah—kindly disposed?

Old Man

That is characteristic of slaves, and luck for you.

Orestes

How would you suggest my getting close to him?

Old Man

Walk past where he will see you as he sacrifices.　　　　635

Orestes

He has his fields, I gather, right beside this road?

Old Man

And when he sees you he will ask you to join the feast.

Orestes

He shall find a bitter banquet-fellow, if god wills.

Old Man

What happens next—you play it as the dice may fall.

Orestes

Well spoken. The woman who gave me birth is—where?　　　　640

Old Man

In Argos. She will join her husband for the feast.

Orestes

But why did she—my mother—not start out with him?

Old Man

The gossip of the crowd disturbs her. She held back.

Orestes

Of course. She feels the city watching her on the sly.

Old Man

That's how it is. Everyone hates a promiscuous wife.   645

Orestes

Then how can I kill them both at the same time and place?

                              (Electra comes forward.)

Electra

I will be the one to plan my mother's death.

Orestes

Good—then fortune will arrange the first death well.

Electra

Let our single friend here help us with both deaths.

Old Man

It shall be done. What death have you decided for her?   650

Electra

Old uncle, you must go to Clytemnestra; tell her
that I am kept in bed after bearing a son.

Old Man

Some time ago? or has your baby just arrived?

Electra

    Ten days ago, which days I have kept ritually clean.

Old Man

    And how will this achieve the murder of your mother?   655

Electra

    She will come, of course, when she hears about the birth.

Old Man

    Why? Do you think she cares so deeply for you, child?

Electra

    Yes—and she can weep about the boy's low breeding.

Old Man

    Perhaps. Return now to the goal of your design.

Electra

    She will come; she will be killed. All that is clear.   660

Old Man

    I see—she comes and walks directly in your door.

Electra

    From there she need walk only a short way, to death.

Old Man

    I will gladly die too, when I have seen her die.

Electra

    But first, old man, you ought to guide Orestes down—

Old Man

    Where Aegisthus holds his sacrifices to the gods?   665

Electra

    Then go face my mother, tell her all about me.

Old Man

    I'll speak so well she'll think it is Electra speaking.

Electra (to Orestes)

    Your task is ready. You have drawn first chance at murder.

Orestes

    Well, I would go if anyone could show me where.

Old Man

    I will escort you on your way with greatest joy.   670

Orestes

    O Zeus of Our Fathers, now be Router of Foes.

Electra

    Have pity on us, for our days are piteous.

Old Man

    Pity them truly—children sprung of your own blood.

Electra

    O Hera, holy mistress of Mycenae's altars—

Orestes

    Grant us the victory if our claim to victory is just.   675

Old Man

    Grant them at last avenging justice for their father.

Electra

    O Earth, ruler below, to whom I stretch my hands—

Orestes

    And you, O Father, dwelling wronged beneath the earth—

Old Man

    Protect, protect these children here, so dearly loved.

Electra

    Come now and bring as army all the dead below—   680

Orestes

    Who stood beside you at Troy with the havoc of their spears—

Old Man

    All who hate the godless guilty defilers here.

Electra

    Did you hear us, terrible victim of our mother's love?

Old Man

    All, your father hears all, I know. Time now to march.

Electra

    I call to you again and say *Aegisthus dies!*   685
    And if Orestes in his struggle falls to death
    I too am dead, let them no longer say I live,
    for I will stab my belly with a two-edged sword.
      I will go in and make our dwelling fit for the outcome:
    then if a message of good fortune comes from you   690
    the whole house shall ring out in triumph. If you die
    triumph will shift to desolation. This is my word.

Orestes

    I understand you.

Electra

                Make yourself fit man for the hour.
    You, my women, with your voices light a fire-
    signal of shouting in this trial. I shall stand guard,   695
    a sword raised ready for the issue in my hand.
    Even in defeat I shall not grant to those
    I hate, the right to violate my living flesh.

                (*Orestes, the Old Man, and Pylades go off toward
                    Mycenae; Electra withdraws into the house.*)

Chorus

The ancient tale is told
    in Argos
still—how a magic lamb   700
from its mother gay on the hills
Pan stole, Pan of the wild
beasts, kind watcher, Pan
who breathes sweet music to his jointed reed.
He brought it to show the gold   705
curls of its wool. On the stone
steps a standing herald called:
To the square, to the square, you men
of Mycenae! Come, run, behold
    a strange and lovely thing   710
for our blessed kings. Swiftly the chorus in dance
    beat out honor to Atreus' house.

The altars spread their wings
    of hammered
gold, fire gleamed in the town
like the moon on Argos' stones   715
of sacrifice, lotus flutes
tended the Muses, lilting
ripples of tune. The dance swelled in desire
tense for the lamb of gold—
whose? Quick, Thyestes' trick:
seducing in the dark of sleep   720
Atreus' wife, he brought
the strange lamb home, his own.
    Back to the square he calls
all to know how he holds the golden beast,
    fleece and horn, from Atreus' house.   725

That hour—that hour Zeus
changed the stars on their blazing course,
utterly turned the splendid sun,

turned the white face of the dawn   730
so the sun drives west over heaven's spine
    in glowing god-lit fire,
the watery weight of cloud moves north,
the cracked waste of African Ammon
dries up, dies, never knowing dew,   735
robbed of the beautiful rain that drops from Zeus.

Thus it is always told.
I am won only to light belief
that the sun would swerve or change his gold
chamber of fire, moved in pain   740
at sorrow and sin in the mortal world,
    to judge or punish man.
Yet terrible myths are gifts
which call men to the worship of god.
You lost god when you killed your lord,   745
forgot the gods and the blood of your glorious brothers.

Listen, listen.
Friends, did you hear a shout? or did anxiety
trick me? a shout deep-rolling like the thunder of Zeus?
Again it comes! The rising wind is charged with news.
Mistress, come out! Electra, leave the house!   750

(*Electra appears at the door.*)

Electra

Dear friends, what is it? How do we stand now in our trial?

Chorus

I do not know yet—only a voice is crying death.

Electra

I hear it too. It is still faint, far. But I hear it.

Chorus

It comes from a great distance, yet it seems so close.

Electra

It is the Argives groaning there—or is it our friends?   755

Chorus

I cannot tell; the note of clamoring is slurred.

Electra

So you announce my death by sword. Why am I slow?

Chorus

Lady, hold back until you learn the outcome clearly.

Electra

Not possible. We are beaten. Where are the messengers?

Chorus

They will come soon. To kill a king is not quick or light.   760

(*Enter a Messenger in excitement.*)

Messenger

Hail maidens of Mycenae, beautiful in triumph!
Orestes is victor! I proclaim it to all who love him.
The murderer of Agamemnon lies on the earth
crumpled in blood, Aegisthus. Let us thank the gods.

Electra

Who are you? Why should I think your message is the truth?   765

Messenger

You do not know your brother's servant? You have seen me.

Electra

Dearest of servants! out of fear I held my eyes
shaded from recognition. Now indeed I know you.
What was your news? my father's hated murderer dead?

Messenger

Dead, dead. I will say it twice if that is pleasing.   770

Electra

O gods! O Justice watching the world, you have come at last.
How did he die? what style of death did Orestes choose,
to kill Thyestes' son? Give me the details.

Messenger

When we rose from your cottage and walked down the hill
we came across a beaten double wagon-track,   775
and there we found the famous master of Mycenae.
He happened to be walking in the water-meadow,
scything young green shoots of myrtle for his hair.
He saw us and called out: "You are most welcome, strangers.
Who are you? Have you traveled far? Where is your home?"   780
Orestes answered, "We are Thessalians on our way
toward Alpheus' valley where we shall sacrifice to Zeus
of Olympia." When Aegisthus heard, he called again,
"Now you must stop among us as our guests and share
our feast. I am at the moment slaughtering a bull   785
for the Nymphs. Tomorrow morning you shall rise refreshed
and lose no time on the road. Come with me to the shrine—"
while he was still talking he took him by the hand
and led us off the road—"I will take no refusal."
When we had reached his garden hut he gave commands: 790
"Quick, someone fill a bowl of water for the strangers
so their hands will be clean to make lustration at the altar."
But Orestes interrupted: "We are clean enough.
We washed ourselves just now in the clear river water.
If citizens need strangers for your sacrifice   795
we are here, Aegisthus. We shall not refuse you, prince."
     After this they broke off public conversation.
Now the king's bodyguard laid down their spears
and sprang all hands to working.
Some brought the lustral bowl and baskets of holy grain,   800
some laid and lit the fire or around the hearth
set up the sacred ewers—the whole roof rang with sound.
Your mother's lover took the barley in his hands

and cast it on the altar as he said these words:
"Nymphs of the Rocks, I have killed many bulls for you,   805
and my wife, Tyndareus' child, has killed often at home.
Guard us in present fortune, ruin our enemies."
(Meaning you and Orestes.) But my master prayed
the utter reverse, keeping his words below his breath,
to take his dynastic place again. Aegisthus raised   810
the narrow knife from the basket, cut the calf's front lock,
with his right hand dedicated it to the holy fire,
and, as his servants hoisted the beast upon their shoulders,
slashed its throat.

     Now he turns to your brother and says,
"One of your great Thessalian virtues, as you boast,   815
is to be a man of two skills: disjointing bulls
and taming horses. Stranger, take the iron knife,
show us how true Thessalian reputation runs."
Orestes caught the beautifully tempered Dorian blade,
loosened his brooch, flung his fine cloak back from his shoulders,   820
chose Pylades as his assistant in the work,
and made the men stand off. Holding the beast by its foot,
he laid the white flesh bare with one pass of his hand.
He stripped the hide off whole, more quickly than a runner
racing could double down and back the hippodrome course,   825
and loosened the soft belly. Aegisthus scooped the prophetic
viscera up in his hands.

    The liver lobe was not
there. Unhidden, the portal-vein and gall-sac showed
disaster coming at him even as he peered.
His face darkened, drew down. My master watched and asked,   830
"What puts you out of heart?" "Stranger, I am afraid.
Some ambush is at my door. There is a man I hate,
an heir to Agamemnon and his war on my house."
He answered, "You can scarcely fear a fugitive's
tricks when you control the state? Now to appease us   835
with sacrificial flesh, will someone bring a knife—
Phthian, not Dorian—and let me split his breast?"

He took it and struck. Aegisthus heaped the soft parts, then
sorted them out. But while his head was bent above them,
your brother stretched up, balanced on the balls of his feet,   840
and smashed a blow to his spine. The vertebrae of his back
broke. Head down, his whole body convulsed, he gasped
to breathe, writhed with a high scream, and died in his blood.

The servingmen who saw it flashed straight to their spears,
an army for two men to face. And yet with courage   845
they stood, faced them, shook their javelins, engaged—
both Pylades and Orestes, who cried, "I have not come
in wrath against this city nor against my people.
I have only paid my father's killer back in blood.
I am injured Orestes—do not kill me, men   850
who helped my father's house of old."

They, when they heard
his words, lowered their spears, and he was recognized
by some old man who used to serve the family.
Swiftly they crowned your brother's head with flower wreaths,
shouting aloud in joy and triumph. He comes to you   855
bringing a head to show you—not a Gorgon horror,
only Aegisthus whom you loathe, who was in debt
for blood and found the paying bitter at his death.

Chorus

Come, lift your foot, lady, to dance
    now like a fawn who in flying   860
arcs leaps for joy, light, almost brushing the sky.
    He wins a garland of glory
more great than those Alpheus' glades grant to the perfect,
your own brother; now, in the hymn strain,
praise the fair victor, chant to my step.   865

Electra

O flame of day and sun's great chariot charged with light,
O earth below and dark of night where I watched before,
my eyes are clear now, I can unfold my sight to freedom,

now that Aegisthus, who had killed my father, falls.
Bring me my few belongings, what my house keeps treasured   870
as ornaments of splendor for the hair, dear friends,
for I will crown my brother as a conqueror.

Chorus

Lay now the bright signs of success
    over his brow, as we circle
our chorused step, dancing to the Muses' delight.   875
    Now again in our country
our old and loved kings of the blood capture the power,
in high justice routing the unjust.
Raise to the flute's tune shouts of our joy.

(Enter Orestes, Pylades, and servants with corpse.)

Electra

O man of triumph sprung of our triumphant father   880
who fought and won below the walls of Troy—Orestes!
Take from my hands these twisted lock-rings for your hair.
You come, a runner in no trifling race, but long
and challenging, to your home goal, killing Aegisthus
who was your enemy, who once destroyed our father.   885
    And you, companion of the shield, Pylades, son
of a most reverend father, please receive your crown
from my hand, for you have won an equal share of glory
in this stark trial. May I see your fortune always high.

Orestes

You must believe, Electra, that the gods have been   890
first founders of our luck; then you may turn to praise
me as the simple servant of both god and luck.
I come to you the killer of Aegisthus, not
in words but action. You know this, but more than this
I have here in my hands the man himself, though dead.   895
You may want to display him for the beasts to eat
or as a toy for carrion birds born of bright air
or stick his head upon a stake. He is all yours.

Electra

I am ashamed to speak and yet I wish to speak.   900

Orestes

What is it? Speak your mind and so emerge from fear.

Electra

I am ashamed to insult the dead; some hate may strike me.

Orestes

There is no man on earth, nor will be, who could blame you.

Electra

Our state is harsh to please and takes delight in slander.

Orestes

Speak as you need to, Sister. We were joined to him   905
in bonds of hatred which could know no gentle truce.

Electra

So be it.
            Which of our sufferings shall I speak in prelude,
which shall I make finale, or marshal in the center?
And yet through rising nights I never once have missed
calling aloud what I wished to tell you to your face   910
if only I were liberated from my fears
of old. We are at the point now. I give you the full
tale of ruin I hoped to tell you in your life.

       You killed me, orphaned me, and him too, of a father
we loved dearly, though he had done no harm to you.   915
In ugliness you bedded my mother, killed her man
who captained the Greeks abroad while you skulked far from
       Phrygia.
You climbed such heights of stupidness that you imagined
your marriage to my mother would not marry you
to cuckoldry, though your own success in Father's bed   920

was criminal. You should know, when a man seduces another's
wife in secret sex and then is forced to keep her,
he heads for disaster if he thinks that she, unchaste
to her first husband, will suddenly turn chaste for him.

Your household life was painful though you could not see it;   925
you knew in your heart that you had made a godless marriage,
and Mother knew she had acquired a godless man,
so each in working pain shouldered the other's load
for mutual help: she got your evil, you got hers.
Every time you walked outdoors in Argos, you heard,   930
"There goes the queen's husband." It was never "the king's wife."
O what perversion, when the woman in the house
stands out as master, not the man. I shake in hate
to see those children whom the city knows and names
not by their father's name but only by their mother's.   935
It marks the bridegroom who has climbed to a nobler bed;
when no one mentions the husband, everyone knows the wife.

Where you were most deceived in your grand unawareness
was your boast to be a man of power since you had money.
Wealth stays with us a little moment if at all;   940
only our characters are steadfast, not our gold,
for character stays with us to the end and faces
trouble, but wealth which lives with us on terms of crime
wings swiftly from the house after brief blossoming.

The women in your life I will not mention—a maiden   945
ought not—but only hint that I know all about them.
You played it haughty since you lived in a grand palace
and were handsome enough. But let me have a husband
not girlish-faced like you but graceful in male courage
whose sons would cling bold to the craggy heights of war;   950
your looks were only ornamental at the dance.

Die then. You paid your debt, never knowing that time
stripped your disguises bare. So should no criminal
who starts his race without a stumble vainly believe
that he has outrun Justice, till in the closing stretch   955
he nears the finish line and gains the goal of death.

Chorus

He wrought horrors, yet has paid in horror to you
and your brother. Justice has enormous power.

Electra

Enough now. Women, take his body out of sight,
conceal it well in darkness so that when she comes   960
my mother sees no corpses till her throat is cut.

(*The corpse is carried into the cottage.*)

Orestes

Hold off a little; we might find another plan.

Electra

What's there? I see some allies racing from Mycenae.

Orestes

Not allies. You are looking at my mother who bore me.

Electra

How beautifully she marches straight into our net;   965
see how grandly she rides with chariot and escort.

Orestes

What—what is our action now toward Mother? Do we kill?

Electra

Don't tell me pity catches you at the sight of her.

Orestes

O god!
How can I kill her when she brought me up and bore me?

Electra

Kill her just the way she killed my father. And yours.   970

Orestes

O Phoebus, your holy word was brute and ignorant.

Electra

Where Apollo is ignorant shall men be wise?

Orestes

He said to kill my mother, whom I must not kill.

Electra

Nothing will hurt you. You are only avenging Father.

Orestes

As matricide I must stand trial. I was clean before.   975

Electra

Not clean before the gods, if you neglect your father.

Orestes

I know—but will I not be judged for killing Mother?

Electra

And will you not be judged for quitting Father's service?

Orestes

A polluted demon spoke it in the shape of god—

Electra

Throned on the holy tripod? I shall not believe you.   980

Orestes

And I shall not believe those oracles were pure.

Electra

You may not play the coward now and fall to weakness.
Go in. I will bait her a trap as she once baited one
which sprang at Aegisthus' touch and killed her lawful husband.

Orestes

I am going in. I walk a cliff-edge in a sea   985
of evil, and evil I will do. If the gods approve,
let it be so. This game of death is bitter, and sweet.

*(Orestes goes slowly into the house with Pylades, without looking back.
Up the road by which he had just come with Aegisthus' corpse, enter Clytemnestra in a chariot, attended by Trojan slave girls.)*

Chorus

> Hail! hail!
> Queen and mistress of Argos, hail,
>   Tyndareus' child,
> sister in blood to the lordly sons   990
> of Zeus who dwell in starred and flaming
> air, saviors adored by men
>   in the roar of the salt sea.
> Hail! I honor you like the gods
> for your looming wealth and brilliant life.   995
> The time to guard and heal your doom
>   is now, O Queen. Hail!

Clytemnestra

> Get out of the carriage, Trojan maidens; hold my hand
> tight, so I can step down safely to the ground.

                    (Looking around somewhat embarrassed.)

> Mostly we gave the houses of our gods the spoils   1000
> from Phrygia, but these girls, the best in Troy, I chose
> to ornament my own house and replace the child
> I lost, my loved daughter. The compensation is small.

Electra

> Then may not I, who am a slave and also tossed
> far from my father's home to live in misery,   1005
> may I not, Mother, hold your most distinguished hand?

Clytemnestra

> These slaves are here to help me. Do not trouble yourself.

Electra

> Why not? You rooted me up, a casualty of war;
> my home was overpowered; I am in your power,
> as they are too—left dark, lonely, and fatherless.   1010

Clymnestra

And dark and lonely were your father's plots against
those he should most have loved and least conspired to kill.
I can tell you—no. When a woman gets an evil
reputation she finds a bitter twist to her words.
This is my case now, not a pretty one. And yet,   1015
if you have something truly to hate, you ought to learn
the facts first; then hate is more decent. But not in the dark.

My father Tyndareus gave me to your father's care,
not to kill me, not to kill what I bore and loved.
And yet he tempted my daughter, slyly whispering   1020
of marriage with Achilles, took her from home to Aulis
where the ships were stuck, stretched her high above the fire
and, like pale field grass, slashed Iphigenia's throat.
If this had been to save the state from siege and ruin,
if it had helped his home and spared his other children   1025
to rack one girl for many lives, I could have forgiven.
But now for the sake of Helen's lust and for the man
who took a wife and could not punish her seducer—
for their lives' sake he took the life of my dear child.
I was unfairly wronged in this, yet not for this   1030
would I have gone savage so, nor killed my husband so,
but he came home to me with a mad, god-filled girl
and introduced her to our bed. So there we were,
two brides being stabled in a single stall.

Oh, women are fools for sex, deny it I shall not.   1035
Since this is in our nature, when our husbands choose
to despise the bed they have, a woman is quite willing
to imitate her man and find another friend.
But then the dirty gossip puts us in the spotlight;
the guilty ones, the men, are never blamed at all.   1040
If Menelaus had been raped from home on the sly,
should I have had to kill Orestes so my sister's
husband could be rescued? You think your father would
have borne it? He would have killed me. Then why was it fair
for him to kill what belonged to me and not be killed?   1045

I killed. I turned and walked the only path still open,
straight to his enemies. Would any of his friends
have helped me in the task of murder I had to do?
    Speak if you have need or reason. Fight me free;
demonstrate how your father died without full justice.   1050

Chorus

Justice is in your words but justice can be ugly.
A wife should give way to her husband in all things
if her mind is sound; if she refuses to see this truth
she cannot enter fully counted to my thought.

Electra

Keep in mind, Mother, those last words you spoke,   1055
giving me license to speak out freely against you.

Clytemnestra

I say them once again, child; I will not deny you.

Electra

But when you hear me, Mother, will you hurt me again?

Clytemnestra

Not so at all. I shall be glad to humor you.

Electra

Then I speak—and here is the keynote of my song.   1060
Mother who bore me, how I wish your mind were healthy.
Although for beauty you deserve tremendous praise,
both you and Helen, flowering from a single stalk,
you both grew sly and lightweight, a disgrace to Castor.
When she was raped she walked of her own will to ruin,   1065
while you brought ruin on the finest man in Greece
and screened it with the argument that for your child
you killed your husband. The world knows you less well than I.
    You, long before your daughter came near sacrifice,
the very hour your husband marched away from home,   1070

were setting your brown curls by the bronze mirror's light.
Now any woman who works on her beauty when her man
is gone from home indicts herself as being a whore.
She has no decent cause to show her painted face
outside the door unless she wants to look for trouble. 1075
  Of all Greek women, you were the only one I know
to hug yourself with pleasure when Troy's fortunes rose,
but when they sank, to cloud your face in sympathy.
You needed Agamemnon never to come again.
And yet life gave you every chance to be wise and fine. 1080
You had a husband scarcely feebler than Aegisthus,
whom Greece herself had chosen as her king and captain;
and when your sister Helen—did the things she did,
that was your time to capture glory, for black evil
is outlined clearest to our sight by the blaze of virtue. 1085
  Next. If, as you say, our father killed your daughter,
did I do any harm to you, or did my brother?
When you killed your husband, why did you not bestow
the ancestral home on us, but took to bed the gold
which never belonged to you to buy yourself a lover? 1090
And why has *he* not gone in exile for your son
or died to pay for me who still alive have died
my sister's death twice over while you strangle my life?
If murder judges and calls for murder, I will kill
you—and your own Orestes will kill you—for Father. 1095
If the first death was just, the second too is just.

Clytemnestra

My child, from birth you always have adored your father. 1102
This is part of life. Some children always love
the male, some turn more closely to their mother than him.
I know you and forgive you. I am not so happy 1105
either, child, with what I have done or with myself.
  How poorly you look. Have you not washed? Your clothes are
    bad.
I suppose you just got up from bed and giving birth?

O god, how miserably my plans have all turned out.
Perhaps I drove my hate too hard against my husband.   1110

Electra

Your mourning comes a little late. There is no cure.
Father is dead now. If you grieve, why not
recall the son you sent to starve in foreign lands?

Clytemnestra

I am afraid. I have to watch my life, not his.
They say his father's death has made him very angry.   1115

Electra

Why do you let your husband act like a beast against us?

Clytemnestra

That is his nature. Yours is wild and stubborn too.

Electra

That hurts. But I am going to bury my anger soon.

Clytemnestra

Good; then he never will be harsh to you again.

Electra

He has been haughty; now he is staying in my house.   1120

Clytemnestra

You see? you want to blow the quarrel to new flames.

Electra

I will be quiet; I fear him—the way I fear him.

Clytemnestra

Stop this talk. You called me here for something, girl.

Electra

I think you heard about my lying-in and son.
Make me the proper sacrifice—I don't know how—   1125

as the law runs for children at the tenth night moon.
I have no knowledge; I never had a family.

Clytemnestra

This is work for the woman who acted as your midwife.

Electra

I acted for myself. I was alone at birth.

Clytemnestra

Your house is set so desolate of friends and neighbors?   1130

Electra

No one is willing to make friends with poverty.

Clytemnestra

Then I will go and make the gods full sacrifice
for a child as law prescribes. I give you so much
grace and then pass to the meadow where my husband rests
praying to the bridal Nymphs. Servants, take the wagon,   1135
set it in the stables. When you think this rite
of god draws to an end, come back to stand beside me,
for I have debts of grace to pay my husband too.

Electra

Enter our poor house. And, Mother, take good care
the smoky walls put no dark stain upon your robes.   1140
Pay sacrifice to heaven as you ought to pay.

> (*Clytemnestra walks alone into the house; the
> Trojan girls withdraw with the chariot.*)

The basket of grain is raised again, the knife is sharp
which killed the bull, and close beside him you shall fall
stricken, to keep your bridal rites in the house of death
with him you slept beside in life. I give you so   1145
much grace and you shall give my father grace of justice.

> (*Electra goes into the cottage.*)

« 57 »

Chorus

    Evils are interchanging. The winds of this house
    shift now to a new track. Of old in the bath
    my captain, mine, fell to his death;
    the roof rang, the stone heights of the hall echoed loud   1150
    to his cry: "O terrible lady, will you kill me now
    newly come home to love at the tenth cycle of seed?"

. . . .

    Time circles back and brings her to the bar,   1155
    she pays grief for love errant. She, when her lord
    came safe home, after dragging years,
    where his stone Cyclops' walls rose straight to the sky, there with
        steel
    freshly honed to an edge killed him, hand on the ax. O wretched   1160
    husband, most wretched suffering must have turned her then:
    a lioness mountain-bred, ranging out
    from her oak-sheltered home, she sprang. It was done.

Clytemnestra (*from inside the house*)

    O children—O my god—do not kill your mother—no.   1165

Chorus

    Do you hear her cry trapped in the walls?

Clytemnestra

    O, O, I am hurt—

Chorus

    I also am hurt to hear you in your children's hands.
    Justice is given down by god soon or late;
    you suffer terribly now, you acted terribly then   1170
    against god and love.

      (*Orestes, Electra, and Pylades emerge from the house, and the
          doors open to reveal the corpses of Aegisthus and
             Clytemnestra lying together.*)

Behold them coming from the house in robes of blood
newly stained by a murdered mother, walking straight,
living signs of triumph over her frightful cries.
There is no house, nor has there been, more suffering   1175
or more at war than this, the house of Tantalus.

Orestes

O Earth and Zeus who watch all work
men do, look at this work of blood
and corruption, two bodies in death
lying battered along the dirt   1180
under my hands, only to pay
for my pain.

Electra

Weep greatly for me, my brother, I am guilty.
A girl flaming in hurt I marched against
  the mother who bore me.

Chorus

Weep for destiny; destiny yours   1185
to mother unforgettable wrath,
to suffer unforgettable pain
beyond pain at your children's hands.
You paid for their father's death as the law asks.

Orestes

Phoebus, you hymned the law in black   1190
melody, but the deed has shone
white as a scar. You granted us rest
as murderers rest—to leave the land
of Greece. But where else can I go?
What state, host, god-fearing man   1195
will look steady upon my face,
  who killed my mother?

Electra

O weep for me. Where am I now? What dance—
what wedding may I come to? What man will take
   me bride to his bed?   1200

Chorus

Circling, circling, your wilful mind
veers in the blowing wind and turns;
you think piously now, but then
thoughtless you wrought an impious thing,
dear girl, when your brother's will was against you.   1205

Orestes

You saw her agony, how she threw aside her dress,
how she was showing her breast there in the midst of death?
   My god, how she bent to earth
the legs which I was born through? and her hair—I touched it—

Chorus

I know, I understand; you have come   1210
through grinding torment hearing her cry
   so hurt, your own mother.

Orestes

She cracked into a scream then, she stretched up her hand
toward my face: "My son! Oh, be pitiful my son!"   1215
   She clung to my face,
suspended, hanging; my arm dropped with the sword—

Chorus

Unhappy woman—how could your eyes
bear to watch her blood as she fought
   for her breath and died there?   1220

Orestes

I snatched a fold of my cloak to hood my eyes, and, blind,
   took the sword and sacrificed
my mother—sank steel to her neck.

Electra

I urged you on, I urged you on,
I touched the sword beside your hand.   1225

Chorus

Working a terrible pain and ruin.

Orestes

Take it! shroud my mother's dead flesh in my cloak,
    clean and close the sucking wounds.
You carried your own death in your womb.

Electra

Behold! I wrap her close in the robe,   1230
the one I loved and could not love.

Chorus

Ending your family's great disasters.

(*The Dioscuri appear on the roof over the scene of mourning.*)

Whom do I see high over your house
shining in radiance? Are they divinities
or gods of the heavens? They are more than men   1235
in their moving. Why do they come so bright
    into the eyes of mortals?

Dioscuri (*Castor speaking for both*)

O son of Agamemnon, hear us: we call to you,
the Twins, born with your mother, named the sons of Zeus,
I Castor, and my brother Polydeuces here.   1240
We come to Argos having turned the rolling storm
of a sea-tossed ship to quiet, when we saw the death
of this our murdered sister, of your murdered mother.
Justice has claimed her but you have not worked in justice.
As for Phoebus, Phoebus—yet he is my lord,   1245
silence. He knows the truth but his oracles were lies.

Compulsion is on us to accept this scene, on you
to go complete the doom which fate and Zeus decreed.
    Give Pylades Electra as a wife in his house,
and leave Argos yourself. The city is not yours   1250
to walk in any longer, since you killed your mother.
The dreadful beast-faced goddesses of destiny
will roll you like a wheel through maddened wandering.
But when you come to Athens, fold the holy wood
of Pallas' statue to your breast—then she will check   1255
the fluttering horror of their snakes, they cannot touch you
as she holds her Gorgon-circled shield above your head.
    In Athens is the Hill of Ares, where the gods
first took their seats to judge murder by public vote,
the time raw-minded Ares killed Halirrhothius   1260
in anger at his daughter's godless wedding night,
in anger at the sea-lord's son. Since then this court
has been holy and trusted by both men and gods.
There you also must run the risk of trial for murder.
But the voting-pebbles will be cast equal and save you,   1265
you shall not die by the verdict: Loxias will take
all blame on himself for having asked your mother's death,
and so for the rest of time this law shall be established:
When votes are equal the accused must have acquittal.
The dreadful goddesses, shaken in grief for this,   1270
shall go down in a crack of earth beside the Hill
to keep a dark and august oracle for men.
Then you must found a city near Arcadian
Alpheus' stream, beside the wolf-god's sanctuary.
and by your name that city shall be known to men.   1275
    So much I say to you. Aegisthus' corpse the men
of Argos will hide, buried in an earth-heaped tomb.
Menelaus will bury your mother. He has come just now
to Nauplia for the first time since he captured Troy.
Helen will help him. She is home from Proteus' halls,   1280
leaving Egypt astern. She never went to Troy.
Zeus fashioned and dispatched a Helen-image there

to Ilium so men might die in hate and blood.
    So. Let Pylades take Electra, girl and wife,
and start his journey homeward, leaving Achaea's lands;   1285
let him also to his Phocian estates escort
your "brother," as they call him—set him deep in wealth.
    Turn your feet toward Isthmus' narrow neck of earth,
make your way to the blessed hill where Cecrops dwells.
When you have drained the fulness of a murderer's doom   1290
you may again be happy, released from these distresses.

Chorus

    Sons of Zeus, does the law allow us
    to draw any closer toward your voice?

Dioscuri

    The law allows, you are clean of this blood.

Electra

    Will you speak to me too, Tyndaridae?   1295

Dioscuri

    Also to you. On Phoebus I place all
      guilt for this death.

Chorus

    Why could you, who are gods and brothers
      of the dead woman here,
    not turn her Furies away from our halls?   1300

Dioscuri

    Doom is compelling, it leads and we follow—
    doom and the brutal song of Apollo.

Electra

    And I? What Apollo, what oracle's voice
    ordained I be marked in my mother's blood?

Dioscuri

> You shared in the act, you share in the fate: 1305
>   both children a single
> curse on your house has ground into dust.

Orestes

> O Sister, I found you so late, and so soon
> I lose you, robbed of your healing love,
> and leave you behind as you have left me.   1310

Dioscuri

> She has a husband, she has a home, she
> needs no pity, she suffers nothing
>   but exile from Argos.

Electra

> Are there more poignant sorrows or greater
> than leaving the soil of a fatherland?   1315

Orestes

> But I go too, I am forced from my father's
> home, I must suffer foreigners' judgment
> for the blood of my mother.

Dioscuri

>   Courage. You go
> to the holy city of Pallas. Endure.   1320

Electra

> Hold me now closely breast against breast,
>   dear Brother. I love you.
> But the curses bred in a mother's blood
> dissolve our bonds and drive us from home.

Orestes

> Come to me, clasp my body, lament   1325
> as if at the tomb of a man now dead.

Dioscuri

>Alas, your despair rings terribly, even
>>to listening gods;
>pity at mortal labor and pain still
>lives in us and the lords of heaven.   1330

Orestes

>I shall not see you again.

Electra

>I shall never more walk in the light of your eye.

Orestes

>Now is the last I can hear your voice.

Electra

>Farewell, my city.
>Many times farewell, fellow citizens.   1335

Orestes

>O loyal love, do you go so soon?

Electra

>I go. These tears are harsh for my eyes.

Orestes

>Pylades, go, farewell; and be kind to   1340
>>Electra in marriage.

Dioscuri

>Marriage shall fill their minds. But the hounds
>are here. Quick, to Athens! Run to escape,
>for they hurl their ghostly tracking against you,
>serpent-fisted and blackened of flesh,   1345
>offering the fruit of terrible pain.
>We two must rush to Sicilian seas,
>rescue the salt-smashed prows of the fleet.

As we move through the open valleys of air
we champion none who are stained in sin, 1350
but those who have held the holy and just
dear in their lives we will loose from harsh
   sorrow and save them.
So let no man be desirous of evil
nor sail with those who have broken their oaths— 1355
   as god to man I command you.

Chorus

   Farewell. The mortal who can fare well,
not broken by trouble met on the road,
   leads a most blessèd life.

THE PHOENICIAN WOMEN

Translated by Elizabeth Wyckoff

INTRODUCTION TO
THE PHOENICIAN WOMEN

THIS is a translation of the play which came down to later antiquity as Euripides' *Phoenician Women*, a play first produced in one of the years 411–409 B.C. What it actually is, is that play, as added to by fourth-century producers. The play in its original form undoubtedly covered, in its episodic action and in its reminiscences of the past and prophecies for the future, more stages of the Oedipus legend than one would have thought a single play could hold. The producers improved on this situation. Their additions brought in everything really memorable in the dramatic tradition of Oedipus which Euripides had left out, drawing freely on earlier plays from the *Seven against Thebes* to the *Oedipus at Colonus*. (This last, of course, Euripides had been unable to draw on, as he died before it was produced.) They also went in for heightening the melodrama, which took some doing.

This has been recognized ever since Valckenaer's edition of 1755, and there are three long passages which modern critics are pretty well agreed in rejecting as the work of Euripides. The first two are easily recognized. One is the messenger's description of the Argive heroes (ll. 1104–40). The second is the report of Eteocles' challenge, and the arming of the brothers for battle (ll. 1221–58). The reader of this translation will not be able to judge the linguistic points which furnish much of the evidence for setting them aside. But I think he can see the extent to which the first is extraneous. Euripides did as much as he wanted to with the Seven in lines 119–81. And the second passage is, among other things, a patchwork of bits from the *Children of Heracles*. These two I have bracketed, to warn the reader.

The third long interpolation begins at line 1582 and may include all the rest of the play.

It seems likely enough that besides the lyric lamentations there was some dialogue between Creon, Oedipus, and Antigone, pointing ahead to the next stages of the story. But the Creon-Oedipus-Antigone scene we have is certainly not the one Euripides wrote.

Note, for one thing, that Antigone is apparently planning both to go into exile, at once, with Oedipus and, in defiance of Creon, to bury Polyneices. This is impossible, but the author is simply assimilating his figure to both Sophoclean Antigones.

However, I am not as sure as some critics are that everything from line 1582 on is invented, or even everything in lines 1582–1709. I think what we may well have here is a Euripidean groundwork, once self-consistent, to which have been added references to those portions of the later story which Euripides chose to omit. (And of course this reworker probably had to do some deleting.) I am unable to disentangle the Euripidean strands in what I suspect to be a collaboration rather than a simple insertion and have therefore bracketed nothing, simply warning the reader here.

Finally, it is obvious that a play which has been so freely handled in gross would probably be tinkered with in detail. This has happened; single lines and short passages have been inserted here and there. For example, line 11 looks very much as if someone wanted to get Creon into the program notes as soon as possible, even though this interrupts Jocasta's identification of herself. Lines 141–44 clear up the sort of point that might have bothered a prompter, and borrow from lines 95–98 to do it. Line 1225 is one of many lines of which the scholiast says, "In many copies this line does not occur." Line 1346 was originally omitted in four manuscripts.

In these, and all analogous cases, I have not troubled the reader with brackets. Editors disagree. However, I have tried to play fair and not to weave an inorganic line into context. Therefore even a reader confined to this translation can join centuries of scholars in spotting the inconsistencies and redundancies. However, he should remember that many of them may well be Euripides' own. Anyone who wishes to pursue these questions further might start with D. L. Page's *Actors' Interpolations in Extant Greek Tragedy* and the Preface to J. U. Powell's edition of this play.

The translation was made from Murray's Oxford text of 1909. The places where I have departed from his readings are these:

Line 22: †(obelus) βρέφος, manuscripts, Murray; λέχος Schoene,
Powell.

Line 1533: ἐπὶ, manuscripts, Murray (who obelizes the passage);
ἐπί "anonymus," quoted by Wecklein, Powell.

Line 1606: I read this as a single line, without the lacuna which
Murray assumes.

Line 1740: I give this line to Oedipus, with the manuscripts and
Powell, rather than to Antigone, with Murray (who had evidence from the scholiast).

THE PHOENICIAN WOMEN

CHARACTERS

Jocasta

Pedagogue

Antigone

Chorus of young women from Phoenicia

Polyneices

Eteocles

Creon

Teiresias

Menoeceus

Two Messengers

Oedipus

THE PHOENICIAN WOMEN

Jocasta

You who cut your way through heaven's stars,
riding the chariot with its welded gold,
Sun, with your swift mares whirling forth our light,
evil the shaft you sent to Thebes that day
when Cadmus came here, leaving Phoenicia's shore,   5
he who wed Cypris' child, Harmonia,
fathering Polydorus, who in turn
had Labdacus, they say, and he had Laius.
Now I am known as daughter of Menoeceus,   10
Creon my brother by the selfsame mother,
my name Jocasta, as my father gave it,
Laius my husband. When he still was childless
after long marriage with me in the palace,
he went to Phoebus asking and beseeching   15
that we might share male children for the house.
But he said, "Lord of Thebes and its famed horses,
sow not that furrow against divine decree.
For if you have a child, him you beget
shall kill you, and your house shall wade through blood."   20
But Laius, in his lust, and drunk beside,
begot a child on me, yet when he had,
knowing his sex was sin, as God had said it,
he gave the child to shepherds to expose   25
in Hera's field, high on Cithaeron's rock,
when he had pinned its ankles with sharp iron
(and this is why Greece called it Oedipus).
Then Polybus' herdsman-riders took the child
and brought it home and gave it to their mistress.
She took my labor's fruit to her own breast   30

and told her husband that it was her own.
When his red beard was growing, my young son,
who had guessed or heard the truth, set off to learn,
at Phoebus' house, his parents. So did Laius,   35
seeking to learn if the child he had exposed
were still alive. They met in middle journey
at the same spot in the split road of Phocis.
Then Laius' runner ordered him away:
"Stranger, yield place to princes." But he came on,   40
silent, in pride. So with their sharp-edged hooves
the mares of Laius bloodied up his feet.
And so—why give the detail of disaster?—
son slew his father, and he took the team
to give to Polybus, his foster parent.
When the Sphinx bore down our city with her raids,   45
my husband gone, Creon proclaimed my marriage:
whoever might guess the clever maiden's riddle,
to him I should be wed. And so it happened.
It was Oedipus, my son, who guessed her song.   50
So he became the ruler of this land
and got the scepter of this realm as prize.
The wretch, unknowing, wedded with his mother;
nor did she know she bedded with her son.
And to my son I bore two further sons,   55
Eteocles and mighty Polyneices,
and daughters two. Her father named Ismene
while I before had named Antigone.
When Oedipus learned I was his wife and mother,
he had endured all suffering, and he struck   60
with terrible gory wounding his own eyes,
bleeding the pupils with a golden brooch.
When his sons' beards had grown, they shut him up
behind the bolts that this fate might be forgotten
which needs too much intelligence to explain it.   65
There in the house he lives, and struck by fate
he calls unholy curses on his children.

They shall divide this house with sharpened steel.
They were afraid that if they lived together   70
the gods might grant his prayers. So they agreed
that Polyneices should go, a willing exile,
while Eteocles stayed in this land and held the scepter,
to change though, year by year. Yet when Eteocles
sat safe on high, he would not leave the throne,
but keeps his brother exiled from this land.   75
He went to Argos, married Adrastus' daughter,
and brings the Argive force he has collected
against these very seven-gated walls,
seeking his share of the land, and his father's scepter.   80
I have persuaded son to come to son
under a truce before they take to arms.
I hope for peace. The messenger says he'll come.
O Zeus who lives in heaven's shining folds
save me and let my sons be reconciled.   85
If you are wise you should not leave a mortal
constantly wretched throughout all of life.

(Jocasta returns to the palace. Enter, from the palace,
Antigone and the old Pedagogue.)

Pedagogue

Antigone, flower of your father's house,
your mother has said you may leave the maiden's room
to climb the very steepest of the roof   90
and see the Argive army, as you asked.
But wait, that I may track the road before you
in case some citizen is in the way.
Then some slight blame would come on me the slave,   95
worse on your highness. Since I know, I'll tell
all that I saw and heard among the Argives
when I went there from here to make the truce
with your brother's army, and came back again.

(The Pedagogue goes up the steps to the house roof.)

No citizen is near the house at all.
Try the old cedar ladder with your feet,   100
look over the plain and see by Ismenus' stream
and Dirce's spring how great the enemy host.

(*Antigone goes up the stairs and speaks at the top.*)

Antigone

Reach your old hand to my young one. Help me step
up from the stairs.   105

Pedagogue (pulling her up)

Take hold, my girl. You're here, but just in time.
The Argive army is moving, the companies part.

Antigone

Hecate, Leto's child! The lightning-shine   110
of bronze all over the plain!

Pedagogue

Polyneices comes no trifler to this land.
He brings the clamor of many horse and foot.

Antigone

The gates, and their locks! Are the brazen bolts
holding firm Amphion's wall of stone?   115

Pedagogue

Take heart, all's well and safe inside the city.
Look at the first man, if you want to mark him.

Antigone

Who is he with the crest of white
who comes at the head of the host and lightly shakes   120
the brazen shield on his arm?

Pedagogue

A captain, lady.

Antigone
>   Yes, but who, and whence?
> Speak out his name, old man.

Pedagogue
> He boasts his birth from Mycenae and he lives   125
> by Lerna's waters, lord Hippomedon.

Antigone
> How prideful, how hateful to see!
> Like an earth-born giant hurling flame in a picture,   130
> not like the race of day.

Pedagogue
> Do you see the one who is crossing Dirce's stream?

Antigone
> How strange, how strange his arms! And who is he?

Pedagogue
> Tydeus, the warrior from far Aetolia.

Antigone
> Is this the one who has married the very sister   135
> of Polyneices' bride?
> How strange his arms, half-barbarous to see!

Pedagogue
> All the Aetolians carry such a shield
> and hurl light lances so they hit the mark.   140

Antigone
> Old man, how did you learn all this so well?

Pedagogue
> I knew them, for I saw their arms before
> when I went from here to there to make the truce
> with your brother's army. I know them in their harness.

Antigone

> Who comes by Zethus' tomb with falling curls,   145
> a youth, and frightful to see?
> Some captain, since an armed crowd follows on.

Pedagogue

> Parthenopaeus, Atalanta's son.   150

Antigone

> I hope that Artemis, ranging the hills with his mother,
> strikes with her shaft and destroys him
> who comes to plunder my town.

Pedagogue

> I hope so, child. But the right is on their side.
> And I am afraid the gods may see things clear.   155

Antigone

> And where is he whom my selfsame mother bore
> to a painful fate?
> Dear ancient, tell me, where is Polyneices?

Pedagogue

> He stands with Adrastus, close by the maidens' tomb,
> Niobe's seven daughters. You see him now?   160

Antigone

> Not clearly, but enough to guess his shape.
> Oh, could I run on my feet like a wind-swift cloud through the
>   sky
> to my own dear brother, and throw my arms round his neck,   165
> poor exile—but how he shines in his golden arms
> ablaze with the light of dawn.

Pedagogue

> He is coming to this house, you may be glad.   170
> Under a truce.

Antigone
>   But who comes here, old man?
> Who mounts and drives a chariot of white?

Pedagogue
> That is the prophet Amphiaraus, lady,
> bringing the victims whose blood shall please this land.

Antigone
> Selene, daughter of shining-girdled Sun,   175
> you with your round gold light, how calm he comes,
> how gently prods his horses!
> —Where is the man who insulted us so fiercely?

Pedagogue
> Capaneus? There he marks the approaches out,   180
> takes the walls' measures up and down the towers.

Antigone
> Nemesis, and you, deep thunder of Zeus,
> and shining flare of the lightning, it is for you
> to put his boasting to sleep.
> He said he would bring the Theban girls   185
> as slaves to Mycenae's women,
> would give them to Lerna's triple fount,
> slaves to Poseidon's lover's waters.
> Artemis, golden-locked, child of Zeus, may I never   190
> endure that slavery.

Pedagogue
> Child, back into the house, and stay inside
> your maiden chamber. You have had the joy
> of that desired sight you wished to see.   195
> Noise in the city proves a crowd of women
> is pressing toward the royal palace now.
> The female sex is very quick to blame.

If one of them gets a little launching place,
far, far she drives. There seems to be some pleasure   200
for women in sick talk of one another.

> (*Antigone and the Pedagogue go into the palace. Enter,*
> *from the side, the Chorus of Phoenician women.*)

Chorus

I came, I left the wave of Tyre
the island of Phoenicia,
as prize for Loxias, slave to Phoebus' house,   205
to rest by Parnassus' snowy ridge.
I came on a ship through the Ionians' sea,
over the fruitless plain,   210
though the west wind rushed from Sicily,
a beautiful blast from heaven.
Chosen most beautiful of my town,
an offering to Apollo,   215
I came to Cadmus' land, as I am Agenor's kin,
sent to Laius' kindred towers.
I might, like the golden statue-girls,   220
have served Phoebus by now.
But Castalia's water is waiting still
to wet my hair for his service.   225

O rock that shines in the fire,
double gleam on the heights
where Dionysus dances,
and vine who distils the daily wealth,   230
the fruitful cluster of grapes,
holy cave of the serpent, mountain rocks
where the gods keep watch, O sacred mountain of snow,
may I, unfearing, dance the Immortal's dance   235
by Phoebus' central hollow with Dirce left behind.

Now before the walls
savage Ares comes   240
kindling the flame of death

for this city—may it not happen.
Shared are the griefs of friends,
shared; if she must suffer,
this seven-gated land, then does Phoenicia share it.   245
Common blood, common children,
through Io who wore the horns.
I also have my part in this.

A cloud about the town,   250
a close cloud of shields,
kindles the scheme of death.
Soon shall Ares know
that he brings to Oedipus' sons
the curse of the very Furies.   255
Ancestral Argos, I fear your strength,
and I fear the gods' part too.
For this man at arms
comes against our home with justice.

(*Enter, from the side, Polyneices, with drawn sword.*)

Polyneices

The warders' bolts have let me through the walls
with ease, and so I fear once in the net
I won't get out unbloodied. Thus I look   265
hither and yonder, watching for a trick.
My hand that holds this sword shall prove my courage.
    Ah, who is there? Or do I fear a noise?
All things seem terrible to those who dare   270
when they set foot upon the enemy's land.
I trust my mother, and I do not trust her
who brought me here under a pledge of truce.
Defense is close. The sacrificial hearths   275
are near, nor is the palace desolate.
I'll thrust my sword in the darkness of its case
and ask who are these women by the house.
    Ladies, what land was it you left to come
to our Hellenic halls?

Chorus

It was Phoenicia reared me. Agenor's grandsons   280
have sent me here a captive, prize for Phoebus.
And while the sons of Oedipus delayed
to send me on to Loxias' oracle
there came the Argives' war against this city.   285
Give answer in return, you who have come
to the gated fortress of the Theban land.

Polyneices

My father is Oedipus, Laius' son, my mother
Jocasta, daughter of Menoeceus.
The Theban people call me Polyneices.   290

Chorus

Kin of Agenor's children who are my lords,
who sent me here—

Master, I fall on my knees,
the humble habit of home.
At last you have come to your father's land.   295
Queen, queen, come forth,
open the gates!
Mother who bore him, do you hear us now?
Why your delay in leaving the halls
and taking your son in your arms?

(*Enter Jocasta from the palace.*)

Jocasta

I heard your Phoenician cry,
girls, and my poor old feet,
trembling, have brought me out.
My child, my child, at last I see you again.   305
Embrace your mother's breast with your arms,
stretch forth your face and your dark curly hair,
to shadow my throat.

Oh, oh, you have barely come,
unhoped for, unexpected, to your mother's arms.   310
What shall I say, how phrase the whole
delight in words and actions
that compasses me about.   315
If I dance in my joy shall I find the old delight?
Child, you went as an exile; your father's house
was left in desolation, your brother's doing.
But your own yearned after you   320
Thebes itself yearned.
And so I weep, and cut my whitened hair.
No longer, child, do I wear white robes,
I have changed to these dark gloomy rags.   325
And the old man in the house, the blind old man,
since the pair of you left the house,
clings to his weeping desire. He seeks the sword   330
for death by his own hand, he casts a noose
over the roof beams mourning his curse on his children.
He is hidden in darkness and steadily wails his woe.   335
And I hear that you have paired yourself in marriage,
the joy of making children.
In a stranger's house you have taken a stranger bride,   340
a curse to your mother and Laius who was of old.
Doom brought by your wedding.
I did not light your wedding torch
as a happy mother should.   345
Ismenus gave no water to the marriage;
your coming to your bride was never sung in Thebes.
May the cause of these sufferings perish, be it the steel 350
or strife, or your father, or a demon-rout
in Oedipus' house.
For all their grief has fallen upon me.

Chorus

Childbirth is terrible for womankind.   355
Therefore all women love their children so.

« 83 »

Polyneices

> Mother, with reason, unreasoning have I come
> among my enemies. But all men must still
> love their own country. Who says something else
> enjoys his talk while thinking far away.   360
> I was so scared, had gone so far in fear
> lest brother's craft might kill me on the way,
> that through the town I came with sword in hand,
> turning my face about. Just one thing helped,   365
> the truce—and your own pledge which led me on
> through the ancestral walls. I came in tears
> seeing at last the halls and the gods' altars,
> the playing fields that reared me, Dirce's spring,
> which I have left unjustly and now live
> in a stranger town, blurring my eyes with tears.   370
> I come from grief and find you grief indeed.
> Your hair is shorn; your garments are of black.
> Alas, alas, my sorrows and myself!
> Mother, how frightful is the strife of kindred,
> and reconciling hard to bring about!   375
> What does my father do within the house,
> he who sees darkness? What of my two sisters,
> do they, poor girls, lament my exile now?

Jocasta

> Some god is ruining all of Oedipus' children.
> The beginning was my bearing outside law.   380
> It was wrong to marry your father and to have you.
> But what of this? The god's will must be borne.
> Still, I must ask you, fearing it may sting,
> one question for whose answer I am yearning.

Polyneices

> Ask openly, leave nothing out at all.   385
> Your wish is mine, my mother.

Jocasta

> So now I ask what first I wish to know.
> What is it to lose your country—a great suffering?

Polyneices

> The greatest, even worse than people say.

Jocasta

> What is its nature? What so hard on exiles?   390

Polyneices

> One thing is worst, a man cannot speak out.

Jocasta

> But this is slavery, not to speak one's thought.

Polyneices

> One must endure the unwisdom of one's masters.

Jocasta

> This also is painful, to join with fools in folly.

Polyneices

> One must be a slave, for gain, against one's nature.   395

Jocasta

> The saying is that exiles feed on hopes.

Polyneices

> Lovely to look at, but they do delay.

Jocasta

> And doesn't time make clear that they are empty?

Polyneices

> They have their charm in troubles.

Jocasta

How were you fed before your marriage fed you?   400

Polyneices

Sometimes I'd have a day's worth, sometimes not.

Jocasta

Your father's foreign friends, were they no help?

Polyneices

Hope to be rich! If you are not—no friends.

Jocasta

Your high birth brought you to no lordly height.

Polyneices

Want's the bad thing. My breeding did not feed me.   405

Jocasta

It seems one's country *is* the dearest thing.

Polyneices

You couldn't say in words how dear it is.

Jocasta

How did you get to Argos, and with what plan?

Polyneices

Apollo gave Adrastus a certain answer.

Jocasta

What sort? Why mention this? I cannot guess.   410

Polyneices

To marry his daughters to a boar and a lion.

Jocasta

What has my son to do with wild beasts' names?

Polyneices

I do not know. He was calling me to my fate.

Jocasta

For the god is wise. How did you meet your marriage?

Polyneices

It was night; I came upon Adrastus' portal.   415

Jocasta

A wandering exile, looking for a bed?

Polyneices

Just so—and then another exile came.

Jocasta

And who was he? Wretched as you, no doubt.

Polyneices

That Tydeus who is named as Oeneus' son.

Jocasta

But why did Adrastus think you were those beasts?   420

Polyneices

Because we fought over the pallet there.

Jocasta

And then he understood the oracle?

Polyneices

And gave us two his daughters two to wed.

Jocasta

Were you happy or unhappy in these weddings?

Polyneices

Right to this day we have no fault to find.   425

Jocasta

How did you lure the army to follow you here?

Polyneices

Adrastus promised his two sons-in-law,
Tydeus and me—Tydeus is now my kinsman—
that both should be brought home, but I the first.
So many Mycenaean chiefs are here   430
and many Danaans, doing me a favor
which hurts me, though I need it. My own town
I fight against. I call the gods to witness
against my will I fight my willing kindred.
But—you can possibly undo these troubles—   435
Mother, you reconcile these kindred-friends,
save you and me and the city from these sorrows.
This has been sung before, but I shall say it:
"Men honor property above all else;
it has the greatest power in human life."   440
And so I seek it with ten thousand spears.
A beggar is no nobleman at all.

Chorus

Here comes Eteocles to hold his parley.
Jocasta, as their mother, it's for you
to say the words to reconcile your sons.   445

                                        (*Enter Eteocles.*)

Eteocles

Mother, I'm here. I came to do a favor
for you. Now what's to come? Let someone speak.
I have broken off my ambushing of chariots
about the walls that I might hear from you
that arbitration for which I have admitted   450
this one within the walls—at your persuasion.

Jocasta

Check for a moment. Swiftness brings not justice.
It is slow speech that brings the greatest wisdom.

Check your dread glare, the seethings of your spirit.
It is not Gorgon's severed head you see; 455
you look upon your brother who has come.
And you, Polyneices, look upon your brother,
for if you look upon his face once more
you will speak better and will hear him better.
I want to give you both some good advice. 460
When friend falls out with friend and they come together
looking at one another, let them look
at that for which they came, forget old wrongs.
Son Polyneices, you may speak the first. 465
For you have come, and brought the Argive army,
as one who claims a wrong. Now may some god
be judge and reconciler of these griefs.

Polyneices

The word of truth is single in its nature;
and a just cause needs no interpreting. 470
It carries its own case. But the unjust argument
since it is sick, needs clever medicine.
I took good foresight for our father's house,
for him, and for myself, hoping to flee
those curses with which once our father cursed us. 475
So willingly myself I left this land,
leaving the rule to him for a year's circle,
so that I myself might take the rule in turn.
Thus we should not fall into hate and envy
doing and suffering evil—but that has happened. 480
For he who swore this, and called the gods to witness,
did nothing of what he promised and still holds
the tyranny and his share of my own house.
And now I am ready, if I get my own,
to send away the army from this land, 485
to take my own house for my proper turn,
and yield it back to him for equal time,
so not to plunder my fatherland nor besiege

her towers with the scaling ladder's steps.
But if I get not justice I shall try   490
to do just this. I call the gods to witness
I have done all in justice, now most unjustly
I am robbed of my fatherland, an offense to heaven.
The facts I've told you, Mother, without heaping
great twists of argument. The clever and the humble   495
alike can see that I have spoken right.

Chorus

I think, though I am not a Hellene born,
that what you say is argued very well.

Eteocles

If all men saw the fair and wise the same
men would not have debaters' double strife.   500
But nothing is like or even among men
except the name they give—which is not the fact.
I'll speak to you, Mother, without concealment:
I'd go to the stars beyond the eastern sky
or under earth, if I could do one thing,   505
seize tyranny, the greatest of the gods.
I will not choose to give this good thing up
to any other, rather than keep it myself.
It's cowardice to let the big thing go
and settle for the smaller. Besides, I should be shamed   510
that he should come in arms and sack the land,
and so achieve his purpose. This would be for Thebes
real shame, if fearing spearmen from Mycenae
I yielded up my scepter for him to hold.
He should not seek his truce with arms in hand,   515
for argument can straighten out as much
as enemy steel can do.
If he will live here on some other terms,
he can. But what he asks I will not yield.
When I can rule should I become his slave?   520

So—on with fire, on with swords of war,
harness the horses, fill the plain with chariots,
knowing that I will never yield my rule.
If one must do a wrong, it's best to do it
pursuing power—otherwise, let's have virtue.   525

Chorus

It isn't right to speak so well of evil.
This is no good thing, but a bitterness to justice.

Jocasta

My son Eteocles, old age is not
a total misery. Experience helps.
Sometimes we can speak wiser than the young.   530
Why do you seek after the goddess Ambition?
The worst of all; this goddess is Injustice.
Often she comes to happy homes and cities,
and when she leaves, she has destroyed their owners,
she after whom you rave. It's better, child,   535
to honor Equality who ties friends to friends,
cities to cities, allies to allies.
For equality is stable among men.
If not, the lesser hates the greater force,
and so begins the day of enmity.   540
Equality set up men's weights and measures,
gave them their numbers. And night's sightless eye
equal divides with day the circling year.
While neither, yielding place, resents the other.   545
So sun and night are servants to mankind.
Yet you will not endure to hold your house
in even shares with him? Where's justice then?
Why do you honor so much tyrannic power
and think that unjust happiness is great?   550
It's fine to be looked up to? But it's empty.
You want to have much wealth within your halls,
much trouble with it?

And what is "much"? It's nothing but the name.
Sufficiency's enough for men of sense.
Men do not really own their private goods;   555
we simply care for things which are the gods',
and when they will, they take them back again.
Wealth is not steady; it is of a day.
Come, if I question you a double question,
whether you wish to rule, or to save the city,   560
will you choose to be its tyrant? But if he wins
and the Argive spear beats down the Theban lance,
then you will see this town of Thebes subdued
and many maidens taken off as slaves,
assaulted, ravished, by our enemies.   565
Truly the wealth which now you seek to have
will mean but grief for Thebes; you're too ambitious.
So much for you.
        Your turn now, Polyneices:
ignorant favors has Adrastus done you,
and you have come in folly to sack your city.   570
Come, if you take this land—heaven forbid it—
by the gods, what trophies can you set to Zeus?
How start the sacrifice for your vanquished country,
and how inscribe your spoils at Inachus' stream?
"Polyneices set these shields up to the gods   575
when he had fired Thebes?" Oh, never, Son,
be this, or such as this, your fame in Greece!
If you are worsted and his side has best,
how shall you go to Argos, leaving here
thousands of corpses? Some will surely say:
"Adrastus, what a wedding for your daughter!   580
For one girl's marriage we have been destroyed."
You are pursuing evils—one of two—
you will lose the Argives or fail in winning here.
Both of you, drop excess. When double folly
attacks one issue, this is worst of all.   585

Chorus

O gods, in some way yet avert these evils
and make the sons of Oedipus agree!

Eteocles

Mother, it's too late for talking, and this intermission time
has been wasted; your good purpose can accomplish nothing now.
For we cannot come to terms except as I have laid them down: 590
that I shall hold the scepter of power in this land.
Leave off your long advisings, now Mother, let me be.
And *you*—outside these walls now, or surely you shall die.

Polyneices

What invulnerable someone will lay a sword on me
for slaughter and not bring away a murder for himself?   595

Eteocles

Near enough, he hasn't left you. Do you see these hands of mine?

Polyneices

Oh, I see you. Wealth's a coward and a thing that loves its life.

Eteocles

Then why come you with so many for a battle with a no one?

Polyneices

Oh, a prudent captain's better than a bad one in the war.

Eteocles

You can boast, when we've a truce that saves you from your   600
death.

Polyneices

So can you. Again I'm claiming rule and sharing of this land.

Eteocles

No use to ask. My house shall still be ruled by none but me.

Polyneices
Holding more than is your sharing?

Eteocles
                                        Yes. Now leave this land at
    once.

Polyneices
Altars of our fathers' worship—

Eteocles
                                        which you come to plunder now

Polyneices
hear me!

Eteocles
                Which of them will hear you when you fight your   605
    fatherland?

Polyneices
Temples of the gods who ride white horses—

Eteocles
                                        and who hate you.

Polyneices
I am driven from my country—

Eteocles
                                for you came to ruin it.

Polyneices
wrongfully, O gods.

Eteocles
                        Don't call on these gods, but Mycenae's!

Polyneices
Impious by nature!

Eteocles
                        Never have I been my country's foe.

Polyneices
who drive me off without my portion.

Eteocles
                                And I'll kill you yet, be-   610
    sides.

Polyneices
Oh, my father, hear my sorrow!

Eteocles
                        And he hears what you are do-
    ing.

Polyneices
and you, Mother!

Eteocles
                It's indecent that you speak of her at all.

Polyneices
O my city!

Eteocles
            Go to Argos, and call on Lerna's stream.

Polyneices
I'm going, never worry. Thank you, Mother.

Eteocles
                                Leave the land!

Polyneices
I am going, but our father, let me see him.

Eteocles
                            You shall not.   615

Polyneices
Or the girls our sisters.

Eteocles
                Never shall you look on them again.

Polyneices (calling)
  O my sisters!

Eteocles
          Now why call them when you are their enemy?

Polyneices
  Fare you very well, my mother.

Jocasta
               Well, I suffer very much.

Polyneices
  I'm no longer son of yours.

Jocasta
             I was born for suffering.

Polyneices
  For this man has done me insult.

Eteocles
             And I stand insulted back.   620

Polyneices
  Where'll you be before the towers?

Eteocles
           And why should you ask
  that?

Polyneices
  I shall stand against, to kill you.

Eteocles
             I desire the selfsame thing.

Jocasta
  Oh, woe is me, my children, what will you do?

Polyneices
                You'll see.

Jocasta

Won't you flee your father's cursings?

Eteocles

          Let the whole house fall
 to ruin.

Polyneices

Soon my bloody sword no longer shall be lazy in its sheath. 625
By the land herself who bore me and her gods I now do swear
that dishonored, badly treated, I am thrust outside the land
like a slave, as if I were not son of Oedipus, as he is.
O my city, if you suffer, lay the blame on him, not me:
I attack against my will, I was thrust away unwilling. 630
Apollo of the roadways and rooftrees, fare you well,
and my friends of youth and statues of the gods we fed with
 honey.
I don't know if I can ever speak a word to you again.
But I still have hope that somehow if the gods are on my side
I shall kill him and be master of this our Theban land. 635

Eteocles

Leave this place; your name means "quarrel" and our father
 named you well.

    (*Jocasta returns to the palace and Polyneices leaves.*)

Chorus

Tyrian Cadmus came to this land.
Here the heifer bent her legs and fell, 640
proved the oracle, told him here to build
his house on the fertile plain,
where comes the moisture of fair-flowing waters, 645
Dirce's water over the furrows green that take the seed,
where his mother bore Bacchus after her marriage with Zeus. 650
He was still a child when the twining ivy came,
green tendrils and all, to cover him over,

to be part of the Bacchic dances of Theban girls 655
and the women who call his name.

And there the bloody dragon was,
savage monster who guarded Ares' spring,
looked with his roving eyes on its running stream.
The beast was slain with a boulder
when Cadmus came seeking water of lustration,
and struck the bloody head with the blows of his monster-slaying
    arm,
sowing its teeth in the furrows deep, at unmothered Pallas' bid-
    ding.
Then earth sent up armed terror over its surface.
Iron-hearted slaughter sent them back again,
and their blood bedewed the land which had briefly showed them
to the shining winds of heaven.

On you also I call, Io's child,
Epaphus, son of our mother, and of Zeus,
—with foreign cry, with foreign prayers— 680
come, come to this land!
It was your descendants who founded it,
and the two-named goddesses own it, Kore and dear Demeter, 685
who is ruler of all, nurse of all, the earth.
Epaphus, send us the goddesses of the torch,
defend this land, for the gods all things are easy.

Eteocles (*to an attendant*)

Go, and bring here Creon, Menoeceus' son, 690
the brother of Jocasta, my own mother,
saying I would consult him on private matters
and state affairs before I go to war.
    But he has saved your trouble; here he is. 695
For now I see him coming to my house.

(*Enter, from the side, Creon.*)

Creon

    I've traveled far, trying to see you, King
    Eteocles; round the Cadmean gates
    and all their guards I went, to hunt you down.

Eteocles

    Creon, be sure I wished to see you too.   700
    I found the terms of peace from Polyneices,
    when we discussed them, far from what we need.

Creon

    I've heard that he desires more than Thebes,
    trusting his new connection and his army.
    But this we must leave hanging on the gods.   705
    I've come to tell you what's immediate.

Eteocles

    What's this? I do not know what you will tell.

Creon

    We have a prisoner from the Argive side.

Eteocles

    What does he say that's new from over there?

Creon

    He says the Argive host will shortly circle,   710
    armor and all, the old Cadmean town.

Eteocles

    Then Cadmus' town must hurry out her arms.

Creon

    But where? Are you too young to see what's needed?

Eteocles

    Over the trenches, where they are to fight.

Creon

This land is few in numbers, they are many.

Eteocles

And well I know that they are bold—in speech.

Creon

Well, Argos has a swelling fame in Greece.

Eteocles

Fear not. I'll fill the plain up with their blood.

Creon

I hope so. But I see much labor here.

Eteocles

So I'll not coop my army within walls.

Creon

To take good counsel—this is victory.

Eteocles

You want that I should turn to other roads?

Creon

All of them, lest our fate depend on one.

Eteocles

Should we lay ambush and attack at night?

Creon

So, if you failed, you would come safe again.

Eteocles

Night holds all even, but favors more the daring.

Creon

It's dread to have ill luck under the darkness.

Eteocles

A spear-attack while they are at their dinner?

Creon

A brief surprise—but we need victory.

Eteocles

But Dirce's stream is deep for their retreat. 730

Creon

Nothing's as good as holding on to safety.

Eteocles

Suppose we rode against the Argive camp?

Creon

They're well walled in, with chariots around.

Eteocles

What shall I do? Give enemies the town?

Creon

No, but take counsel, though you are so clever. 735

Eteocles

And what forecounsel's cleverer than mine?

Creon

They say that seven men, as I have heard—

Eteocles

What's their assignment? This is a small force.

Creon

will lead their companies to assault the gates.

Eteocles

What shall we do? Not wait till I am helpless? 740

Creon

You also choose out seven for the gates.

Eteocles

To take command of troops, or fight alone?

Creon

With troops, when they have chosen out the best.

Eteocles

I see—to ward off scalings of the walls.

Creon

And choose lieutenants; one man can't see all.   745

Eteocles

Choosing for courage or for prudent minds?

Creon

Both. Neither's any good without the other.

Eteocles

So be it. To the seven-gated town
I'll go, and set the captains as you say
in even numbers against their enemies.   750
It would take long, long talk to give each name,
now while the enemy camps outside our walls.
But I will go, my arm shall not be idle.
I hope my brother may be my opponent,
that I may fight and take him with my spear   755
and kill him who came to sack my fatherland.
The marriage of Antigone, my sister,
and your son Haemon, will be your affair
if I should fail. Their earlier betrothal
I ratify, as I move off to war.   760
You are my mother's brother. I need not tell you

to care for her, for my sake and your own.
My father bears the weight of his own folly,
self-blinded. I won't praise this, and his curse
may kill his sons if it is brought to pass.   765
One thing we haven't done. We should find out
if seer Teiresias has some word for us.
I'll send your son Menoeceus after him,
the boy who has your father's name, to bring him.   770
With kindness will he come to speak to you,
but I have blamed his seercraft and he hates me.
I lay one charge on you, and on the city,   775
if our side wins, let never Polyneices
be buried here in Theban earth. If someone
tries burial, he must die, though he be dear.
So much to you. And now to my own followers:
bring out my arms and armor. To the fight
which lies before me now I go with Justice,   780
who will bring victory. And I pray to Prudence,
kindest of gods, that she will save this city.

                                                 (*Exit Eteocles.*)

Chorus

Ares, who brings us trouble, lover of blood and death,
why do you love them, why stand away from Bromios' feasts?   785
Never, when dances are fair and the girls are crowned,
do you loosen your locks and sing to the breath of the flute
which the Graces have given for dancing. No, you rouse the host,
the armed host of Argos against our Thebes with blood.   790
You dance first in the dance that knows no music.
Not when the thyrsus whirls and the fawns are there
do you come to Ismenus' stream.
But with sound of chariots, clatter of bits and hooves,
you urge the Argives against our earth-sown race,   795
a dancing crowd in arms that swells with shields,
decked in bronze to batter our walls of stone.
Strife is a terrible god, she who has planned
these sufferings for our rulers, the Labdacid kings.   800

O glade with the holy foliage, loved by the many beasts,
Artemis' own Cithaeron that wears the snow,
would you had never taken Jocasta's child
and brought to rearing Oedipus, child cast out of his house,
marked by the golden pins. And would that the wingèd maid,   805
the mountain portent of grief had never sung her songs,
the Sphinx whose music was no music at all,
who climbed over our walls with hoof and claw
and dragged our youth on high
to heaven's height untrodden, she whom Hades sent   810
against the people of Cadmus. And another evil strife,
the strife of Oedipus' children, comes on the town and its homes.
Evil is never good, nor are these lawless sons,   815
their mother's travail, their father's shame.
She came to her kinsman's bed. . . .

    [A few words are missing at the end of this antistrophe.]

Earth, you bore, you bore
—I heard the news in my foreign home, I heard it well—
the race that grew from the teeth of the crimson-crested monster,   820
Thebes' noblest shame.
And the sons of heaven they came to Harmonia's marriage,
the walls of Thebes they rose to Amphion's lyre,
midway between the streams   825
which pour their moisture over the rich green plain
from Dirce and Ismenus.
And Io, my hornèd mother, was also mother to kings of Thebes.
This city has shifted from one rule to another, but ever   830
has stood on high, decked with the crowns of war.

                     (*Enter the prophet Teiresias, led by his young
                            daughter, accompanied by Menoeceus.*)

Teiresias

Now lead me on, my daughter. You're the eye
for my blind steps, as star is to a sailor.   835
Now set my path upon the level plain

and lead me lest I stumble. Your father's weak.
Guard my lot-tablets with your maiden hand
which on my holy seat of prophecy   840
I drew when I had marked the oracle-birds.
O young Menoeceus, Creon's son, now tell me,
how far is still our journey to the town,
and to your father? My knees begin to buckle.
I've come so far I hardly can go on.

Creon

Take courage. You have come to harbor now,   845
among your friends. Now hold him up, my son.
Mule cars, and old men's feet, they need the help
of someone else's hand.

Teiresias

Ah, we are here. Why did you want me, Creon?

Creon

I've not forgotten. But collect your strength,   850
and draw your breath; forget your laboring road.

Teiresias

I am fatigued, since only yesterday
I came from labor for Erechtheus' sons.
There they had war against Eumolpus' spear,
and I gave Cecrops' children victory.   855
So, as you see, I wear a golden crown,
as first fruit of their plunder from the foe.

Creon

I'll take your crown of victory as an omen.
We're in mid-wave of danger, as you know,
Danae's sons against us, strife for Thebes.   860
Our king is gone, dressed in his warrior-arms,
against Mycenae's force, Eteocles.

But he enjoined me to find out from you
what we should do in hope to save our city.

Teiresias

As far as he goes, I'd have locked my mouth,   865
withheld the oracles, but at your asking,
I'll tell you. Creon, the land has long been sick,
since Laius made a child against heaven's will,
and begot poor Oedipus, husband to his mother.
The bloody ruin of his peering eyes   870
is the gods' clever warning unto Greece.
And Oedipus' sons who tried to cloak this up
with passage of time, as if to escape the gods,
erred in their folly, since they gave their father
neither his rights nor freedom to depart.   875
And so they stung the wretch to savage anger.
Therefore he cursed them terribly indeed,
since he was ailing and, besides, dishonored.
What did I not do, what did I not say?
All the result was hatred from those sons.
Death by their own hands is upon them, Creon;   880
and many corpses fallen over corpses,
struck with both Argive and Cadmean shafts,
will give the Theban land a bitter mourning.
You, my poor city, will be buried with them,
if no one is persuaded by my words.   885
This would be best, that none of Oedipus' house,
live in the land as citizen or lord,
since the gods hound them on to spoil the state.
But since the bad is stronger than the good
there is one other way to save the town.   890
But even for me it is not safe to say
that which is bitter to the man in power
who yet could save this city. Fare you well.
One among many, I will take what comes.
What else to do?   895

Creon

Stay here, old man.

Teiresias

Do not lay hands on me.

Creon

Now wait! Why flee?

Teiresias

Luck flees you, not myself.

Creon

Speak the salvation of the town and townsmen.

Teiresias

Now you may wish it; soon you'll wish it not.

Creon

I could not fail to wish my country's safety.   900

Teiresias

You really want to hear, and you are eager?

Creon

What should I be more earnest for than this?

Teiresias

Soon you will hear about my prophecies.
—But first there's something that I need to know.
Where is Menoeceus, he who brought me here?   905

Creon

He isn't far away, he's close to you.

Teiresias

Let him withdraw, far from my prophecies.

Creon

He is my son and will not talk at large.

Teiresias

You wish that I should speak while he is here?

Creon

Yes. He'll be glad to hear of what will save us.   910

Teiresias

Then shall you hear the way of prophecy,
what you must do to save the Theban town.
You must kill Menoeceus for his country's sake,
your child—since you yourself have asked your fate.

Creon

What are you saying? What's your word, old man?   915

Teiresias

Just what it is, and this you needs must do.

Creon

Oh, you have said much evil in short time.

Teiresias

Evil to you, great safety to your city.

Creon

I wasn't listening, I didn't hear.
City, farewell.

Teiresias

This is no more the man he was. He dodges.   920

Creon

Go, and goodbye. I do not need your seercraft.

Teiresias

Has truth now died because you are unhappy?

Creon

Oh, by your knees and by your old man's beard—

Teiresias

Why fall before me? What you ask is ruin.

Creon

be quiet; don't reveal this to the town.   925

Teiresias

You tell me to do wrong; I won't keep quiet.

Creon

What will you do? You plan to kill my child?

Teiresias

Others must deal with action. I must speak.

Creon

Why is this curse on me, and on my son?

Teiresias

You are right to ask, and bring me to debate.   930
He must, in that chamber where the earth-born dragon
was born, the watcher over Dirce's streams,
be slaughtered, and so give libation blood
for Cadmus' crime, appeasing Ares' wrath,
who now takes vengeance for his dragon's death.   935
Do this, and Ares will be your ally.
If earth gets fruit for fruit, and human blood
for her own offspring, then this land shall be
friendly to you, she who sent up the crop
of golden-helmeted Sown Men. One of their race,
child of the dragon's jaws, must die this death.   940
You are the one survivor of the Sown,
pure-blooded, on both sides, you and your sons.
Haemon's betrothal saves him from the slaughter.
For he is not unwedded, though still virgin.   945
This boy, who belongs to none but to the city,
if he should die, might save his fatherland,

make harsh homecoming for Adrastus and the Argives,
casting the dark of night upon their eyes,   950
and make Thebes famous. There you have your choice,
to save your city or to save your son.
　　Now you have all I know. Child, take me home.
A man's a fool to use the prophet's trade.
For if he happens to bring bitter news   955
he's hated by the men for whom he works;
and if he pities them and tells them lies
he wrongs the gods. No prophet but Apollo
should sing to men, for he has nought to fear.

　　　　　　　　　(*Exeunt Teiresias and his daughter.*)

Chorus

Creon, why are you silent, holding your tongue?   960
But I myself am stricken and amazed.

Creon

What can one say? But my response is clear.
I'll never walk into such wretchedness
as to give my city the slaughter of my son.
It's part of human life to love one's children.   965
No one would give his own son up to death.
Let no one praise me who would kill my sons!
Though I, since I am in the prime of life,
am ready to die to set the country free.
Up, son, before the whole town learns of this,   970
pay no attention to these wanton bodings,
fly quickly, get yourself outside this land.
For he will tell this to the chiefs and captains
making the rounds of the gates and their commanders.
If we anticipate him, you are safe.   975
If you come second, we're destroyed, you die.

Menoeceus

Where shall I flee, what city and what friend?

Creon

As far away from here as you can get.

Menoeceus

You'd better tell me where, and I will do it.

Creon

Go beyond Delphi—

Menoeceus

and where on beyond? 980

Creon

into Aetolia.

Menoeceus

And where after that?

Creon

Thesprotia's plain.

Menoeceus

Where holy Dodona stands?

Creon

Yes.

Menoeceus

What protection will that be for me?

Creon

The god will guide you.

Menoeceus

And for my supplies?

Creon

I'll give you gold.

Menoeceus

Thank you for that, my father. 985
Go get it then. I'll go to see your sister
Jocasta, she who nursed me at her breast,

« 111 »

when my mother died and I was left an orphan.
I'll go to see her, and I'll save my life.
—Please hurry, Father, *you* don't want to keep me.   990

(Exit Creon. Menoeceus addresses the Chorus.)

Women, how well I've taken away his fear,
cheating with words, to get what I desire.
He'd steal me out, robbing the state of safety,
give me to cowardice. This can be forgiven
an ancient, but not pardoned in myself,   995
that I should so betray my fatherland.
Know well, I'm going, and I'll save the town,
and give my life to death to save the land.
How shameful if men who are not under omens,
and so constrained by heaven's necessity,   1000
stand at their shields and do not shrink at death,
fighting before the towers for fatherland,
while I, betraying my father and my brother
and my own city, leave the land a coward.
Wherever I'd live, I'd show myself a weakling.   1005
By Zeus, among the stars, and bloody Ares,
who set the sprouting offspring of this land
to be its rulers, I am going now.
I'll take my stand on the high battlements
over that precinct where the dragon lived,
there slay myself above its gloomy depths   1010
that the seer spoke of; so I'll free the land.
I've said my say, and now I go to give
my city no mean gift. I'll cure this ailing land.
If every man would take what good he can   1015
and give it to his city's common good,
cities would suffer less, be happy from now on.

(Exit Menoeceus.)

Chorus
    You came, you came,
    you wingèd thing, earth's offspring, monster's child,   1020

to seize the sons of Cadmus.
Half a maiden, a fearful beast,
with roving wings and claws that fed on blood.   1025
You who snatched the youths from Dirce's plain,
crying your Fury's shriek,
the song that knows no music,
you brought, you brought sorrows upon our land,   1030
bloody ones—and bloody was the god
who brought these things about.
Mournings of the mothers,
mournings of the maidens,
filled our homes with grief.   1035
Groan and cry ran back and forth
from one to another through the town,
and thunder groaned as they did   1040
each time the wingèd bird seized one of the city's men.

In time there came
by Pythian sending Oedipus the wretched,
here to this land of Thebes.   1045
Then were we glad, but later we grieved.
He conquered the riddle; poor wretch, he wed his mother.
He stained the town and through slaughter he came to strife,   1050
casting the curse on his sons.
We praise him who goes,
we praise the man who is dying to save his land.   1055
Groaning he leaves to Creon.
But the seven-gated town,
her he makes to conquer.
Pallas, make us mothers   1060
of sons as good as this,
you who checked the dragon-blood,
by the rock you urged Cadmus to throw.
Yet from this saving came   1065
a curse of God on this land, and slaughter with it.

(*Enter, from the side, an armed messenger.*)

Messenger

You there, whoever's watching at the gate,
open, and bring Jocasta from the house.
Open, I say! You've waited long, but now
come forth and hear, famed wife of Oedipus,   1070
leaving your wailing and your tears of grief.

(*Enter Jocasta from the palace.*)

Jocasta

Dear friend, you haven't come to tell disaster,
Eteocles' death, you who march by his shield,
constantly keeping off the enemy shafts.
What is the new word that you bring to me?   1075
Is my son alive or dead? Now tell me true.

Messenger

He lives, so tremble not, that fear is gone.

Jocasta

How is the circuit of the seven gates?

Messenger

They stand unbroken, the city is not plundered.

Jocasta

Were they endangered by the Argive spear?   1080

Messenger

Right on the verge. But our Cadmean Ares
was stronger than the Mycenaean spear.

Jocasta

By the gods, tell one thing more! What do you know
of Polyneices? I care for his life too.

Messenger

Both of your sons are living to this moment.   1085

Jocasta

God bless you! How, when you were sore besieged,
did you force back the Argives from the gates?
Tell me, that I may please the blind old man,
sitting inside, with news of the city's saving.

Messenger

When Creon's son, who died to save the city,   1090
on the highest tower standing, had thrust his sword
through his own throat and saved this land of ours,
your son sent seven companies and their captains,
to the seven gates, to keep the Argives off.
Horses against the horsemen did he set,   1095
foot against infantry, so where the wall
was weak against assault, he guarded it.
From the high citadel we saw the host,
white-shielded men of Argos. They left Teumesus,   1100
they rushed the ditch to set the town on fire.
Then the paean and the trumpet played together,
from there, and from our walls.
[Then first attacked were the Neitian gates
by a company bristling with its thick-set shields.   1105
Parthenopaeus led them, the huntress' child,
whose family sign was blazing on his shield,
Atalanta with her distant-ranging arrows
killing Aetolia's boar. Against the gate
of Proetus, came the man of sacrifice,
carrying victims on his car, no signs   1110
of insolence on his shield. Wisely, his arms were blank.
Against the Ogygian gate the lord Hippomedon
came with a sign in middle of his shield,
the All-Seeing one, with eyes all over him,   1115

some eyes that look forth as the stars come up,
others that hide among the setting stars,
and will look later when that man has died.
Against the next gate Tydeus took his stand.
He bore a lion's hide upon his shield   1120
with bristling mane. And there Prometheus held
in his right hand the torch to burn the town.
Your Polyneices by the Gate of Springs
led on the war. Upon his shield the fillies
of Potniae raged and ran in panic-fear,   1125
worked by the pivots near the handle-grip.
They did seem mad indeed.
And he who loves war even as Ares does
Capaneus led against the Electran gate.
The iron markings on his shield were these: 1130
an earth-born giant carried on his shoulders
a whole town wrenched away from its foundations,
this to suggest what our town is to suffer.
Adrastus himself was at the seventh gate.
A hundred snakes were drawn upon his shield.   1135
Yes, on his left arm rode the Argive Hydra.
And from our walls these snakes, with snatching jaws,
were taking Cadmus' children.
Now all these things I very well could see
since it was I who took the password round.]   1140
So first we fought with arrows and throwing-spears
and far-flung slingshots and the crash of stones.
When we had won this fighting, Tydeus cried,
sudden, so did your son, "O Danaan men,
do not delay, before their shafts have stunned you,   1145
fall on the gates, light-armed, and horse, and chariots."
And when they heard the cry, no man was slow
and many fell, their heads bedaubed with blood.
On our side too you might have seen as many   1150
dive to the plain and breathe their life away.
They dewed the dry earth with their streams of blood.

Then that Arcadian, Atalanta's son,
no Argive, rushed upon the gates a storm,
crying for double-axes and for fire,
meaning to overturn our town, but then   1155
the sea-god's son, Periclymenus, cast a stone,
a wagon's load, from the high cornice-top,
broke up his yellow head, shattered the joinings
of bone on bone; straightway his blushing face   1160
blushed with his blood. He'll not return his life
to the queen of archers, his mother, the mountain maid.
When he had seen that this gate was defended,
your son went on, I followed, and I saw
Tydeus, and many shieldmen him beside   1165
dashing Aetolian spears against the front
of our defenses, so that many fled
the outer battlements. But against him too
your son brought on the crowd as a huntsman does
and saved the towers. So to the next gate   1170
we hurried on, having stopped the sickness there.
How can I tell you how Capaneus raged?
For he came with the steps of a long ladder.   1175
This was his boast, that Zeus's awful fire
could not hold him back from overturning the city.
He cried this as they threw the stones against him,
and still climbed up, cowered within his shield,
step after step, the ladder rung by rung.
Just as he reached the cornice of the wall   1180
Zeus struck with lightning, and the earth rang out
so all were frightened. From the ladder he fell,
limbs whirling like a sling. His hair streamed high;
his blood fell down to earth. His arms and legs
went spinning like Ixion on his wheel.   1185
He fell upon the ground a flaming corpse.
When Adrastus saw Zeus was his enemy,
he drew his army back behind the ditch.
But we, who saw the omen on our side,

horsemen and chariots and foot rushed out.   1190
We crashed our spears into their very center;
ruin was everywhere. They died, they fell
down from the chariot's rim. The wheels rebounded.
Axle on axle, corpse on corpse was heaped.   1195
This land's defenses have been kept from ruin
this day. The gods must see if this our land
shall still be fortunate, for some god has saved her.

Chorus

How fair is victory! If the gods have still   1200
a better plan, I'll hope for my own fortune.

Jocasta

The gods and fortune both have served us well.
My sons are alive. The country has escaped.
But Creon, he has reaped a mournful harvest,   1205
who married me to Oedipus. Gone is his son:
good fortune for the town, a grief to him.
Go on and tell me what my son will do.

Messenger

Let be the rest. So far your fortune holds.

Jocasta

Suspicious sayings. This I'll not allow.   1210

Messenger

What more do you want than to know your sons are saved?

Jocasta

To hear if I have happiness in the future.

Messenger

Let me go. Your son's near helper is not with him.

Jocasta

You hide some evil and cover it up in dark.

Messenger

    I would not add your sorrows to your gains.   1215

Jocasta

    You must, unless you fly away to heaven.

Messenger

    Alas, why not have let me leave good news?
    Why force me to the bad?
    Your sons intend—Oh shamefulness of daring!—
    a single combat, severed from the host.   1220
    [And they have said to Argives and Cadmeans
    words which should never have been said at all.
    Eteocles began. High on a tower,
    he ordered that the army be called to silence
    and said, "O leaders of the land of Hellas,   1225
    lords of the Danaans, you who here have come,
    and Cadmus' people, not for Polyneices
    nor for myself should you exchange your lives.
    For I myself, putting this danger off,
    alone will join in battle with my brother.   1230
    If I kill him, I'll hold my house alone;
    if I am worsted, to him alone I'll yield it.
    Give up the fight, Argives, and leave the land;
    of the Sown Men there are already dead enough.   1235
    So much he said, and your son Polyneices
    straightway leapt up and praised what he had said.
    And all the Argives shouted their approval,
    and Cadmus' people, for they thought it just.
    So truce was made. In no man's land the chiefs   1240
    took solemn oath they would abide by it.
    Then did they cover their bodies with brazen arms,
    the two young sons of the old Oedipus.
    Their friends were dressing them. The Theban lords
    saw to our captain, the Argive chiefs the other.   1245
    Then they stood shining, and they had not paled.

And from about their friends came up to them,
cheered them with speech and said such words as this:
"Polyneices, now you can set up for Zeus   1250
his triumph-statue and make Argos famed."
To Eteocles: "Now you are fighting for your city,
now if you conquer, you will hold the rule."
Such things they said, exhorting them to battle.
The seers slew sheep and marked the points of flame,   1255
its cleavages, any damp signs of evil,
and that high shining which may have two meanings,
a mark of victory, or of the losing side.]
If you have help or any words of wisdom
or spells of incantation, go, hold back   1260
your children from dread strife. The danger's great.
Your dreadful prize will only be your tears
if you should lose both sons this very day.

(Exit the messenger.)

Jocasta
My child Antigone, come outside the house.
No help for you in maidens' works and dances.   1265
The gods have set it so. But those brave men
your brothers, who are rushing on their death,
you and your mother must keep from mutual murder.

(Enter Antigone from the palace.)

Antigone
Mother, what new terror for your own   1270
do you cry out before the palace front?

Jocasta
Daughter, your brothers' lives are falling fast.

Antigone
What do you say?

Jocasta
                    They're set for single fight.

Antigone

What will you tell me?

Jocasta

Hard words. Follow me.

Antigone

Where, as I leave my chamber?

Jocasta

To the armies.   1275

Antigone

I fear the crowd.

Jocasta

Modesty will not help.

Antigone

What shall I do?

Jocasta

Undo your brothers' strife.

Antigone

But how?

Jocasta

Prostrate, with me, before them.

Antigone

Lead, Mother, to the plain. We can't delay.

Jocasta

Then hurry, hurry, daughter. If I catch them   1280
before they hurl their spears, my life's in light.
But if they die, I'll lie with them in death.

(*Exeunt Jocasta and Antigone.*)

Chorus

Alas, alas, my shuddering heart!
Pity, pity goes through my flesh.   1285

as I think of that wretched mother.
Which of her children will kill her child
—Oh, the sufferings, Zeus, Oh earth—   1290
cutting his brother's throat, spilling his brother's breath?
and I, poor soul, which corpse shall I lament?

Woe, oh woe, twin beasts!
Bloody spirits, shaking the spear,
how soon they will work their murders!
Unhappy that ever they came to this duel.   1300
With foreign wailings I'll mourn the dead.
The fortune of death is near, the light will show what comes.
Murder the Furies have wrought is a fate beyond all fates.   1305

But I see Creon coming to the house
with clouded face, and break off this lament.

(Enter, from the side, Creon, and attendants
carrying the body of Menoeceus.)

Creon

What shall I do? And do my tears lament   1310
myself, or this poor city, held in gloom
as if it traveled over Acheron.
My child has perished, dying for the land.
The name he leaves is noble, but sad for me.
Just now I took him from the dragon-rocks,   1315
took in my arms my son who killed himself.
My whole house mourns. And I, in my old age,
I come for my old sister, Queen Jocasta,
to lay my son out for his funeral.
For to the dead we who are not yet dead   1320
should pay respect, honoring the god below.

Chorus

Gone is your sister, Creon, from the house.
And with her went the maid Antigone.

Creon

Where? And what trouble called them? Tell me now.

Chorus

She heard her sons were planning single fight   1325
with spear and shield over the royal house.

Creon

What are you saying? This I had not heard,
since I was caring for my own son's corpse.

Chorus

Your sister left the house some time ago.
I think the mortal combat of those sons,   1330
Oedipus' sons, is at an end by now.

Creon

Alas, indeed I see a sign of that.
The dark and scowling face of one who comes
to bring the news of everything that's happened.

(*Enter a messenger, from the side.*)

Messenger

Woe is me, how tell my story or the groaning that I bring?   1335

Creon

We are ruined, I can tell it from the gloom with which you start.

Messenger

"Woe is me," I cry again, for the trouble I bring is great.

Creon

To be heaped upon the suffering we had suffered. What's your
    news?

Messenger

Creon, your sister's children are no longer in the light.

Creon

Alas!   1340
Great is the sorrow you bring, for me and for the state.
O house of Oedipus, have you heard the news?
Your sons have perished, both in one disaster.

Chorus

The house might weep, if it could understand.

Creon

Alas, disaster, born of heavy fate!   1345
Ah, for my sorrows, how I suffer now!

Messenger

Then do you know the further misery?

Creon

How could there be a worser fate than this?

Messenger

Your sister died along with her two sons.

Chorus

Lead off the wailing, batter your head in mourning   1350
with your fair white arms!

Creon

Jocasta, what an ending to your life,
and to your marriage which that riddle made.
    Tell me about the slaughter of the sons,
the working-out in fight of Oedipus' curse.   1355

Messenger

You know our first good fortune before the towers,
for the girdle walls are not so far away
you couldn't see the things that happened there.

When they were ordered in their shining arms,
the two young sons of Oedipus the old,   1360
they rose and went into the middle plain,
the two commanders, the pair of generals,
for the struggle of the single fight in arms.
Looking toward Argos Polyneices prayed,
"O lady Hera, yours I am, since wed   1365
to Adrastus' child and living in your land.
Grant I may kill my brother, so my hand
show sign of victory, my opponent's blood."
He asked a shameful crown, his brother's death.
Tears came to many at fate's monstrosity.   1370
Men slipped their eyes about among the crowd.
Eteocles prayed, looking toward the house
of golden-shielded Pallas, "Daughter of Zeus,
grant me to cast my spear in victory
against my brother's breast from this my arm,   1375
to kill the one who comes to sack my land."
Then the Tyrrhenian trumpet-blast burst forth,
like fire, as the signal for the fight;
they ran a dreadful race at one another
and like wild boars that sharpen their savage teeth   1380
drew close, both foaming slaver down their beards.
Both shook their spears, but drew within their shields
so that the steel might spend itself in vain.
If either saw the other's eye peer up
above the rim, he darted with his spear,
hoping to catch him quickly with its point.   1385
But both were clever, peering through the shield-slits,
so neither's spear was any use at all.
We who were watching sweated more than they,
all fearful for our friends.
Eteocles slipped a little on a stone
that turned beneath his foot. One leg came out   1390
around the shield; and Polyneices struck,

seeing the mark thus offered to his steel.
The Argive spear went cleanly through his calf
and all the Danaan army cried in joy.
And then Eteocles saw his brother's shoulder
bare in the struggle, and he struck at that.
Thebans rejoiced; the spearhead broke off short.
His spear no use, he fell back step by step,   1400
then seized and hurled a rugged rock which broke
his brother's spear, so now on even terms
they stood, since neither had a lance in hand.
Then snatching at the handles of their swords
they came together, and they clashed their shields,   1405
pushed back and forth, and frightful was the noise.
Eteocles, who'd been to Thessaly,
had learned and used a fine Thessalian trick.
He disentangled from their present struggle,
fell with his left foot back, watching his mark   1410
in his foe's belly. Then he jumped ahead
on his right foot and struck him in the navel.
The sword went through and stuck right in the spine.
Stooped over his belly Polyneices falls   1415
with gasps of blood. The victor stuck his sword
into the earth, began to strip his arms.
Not mindful of himself, only of that.
This was his finish. The other had some life left,
had kept his sword all through his painful fall,   1420
scarcely he managed, but he thrust that sword,
he the first-fallen, through his brother's liver.
They bit the dust and lie near one another;
the two did not divide their heritage.

Chorus

O Oedipus, how much I mourn your woes.   1425
It seems a god has now fulfilled your curse.

Messenger

Hear now the woe that followed upon these.
Just as her fallen children left this life
their mother came upon them in her haste,
she in her hurry, with her daughter too.   1430
And when she saw them with their mortal wounds,
she groaned, "O children, I bring help too late."
Falling upon her children, each in turn,
she wept, she mourned them, all her wasted nursing.
Their sister at her side like a warrior's helper   1435
cried, "O supporters of our mother's age,
you have betrayed my marriage, dearest brothers."
Eteocles' hard dying breath was coming
out from his chest, and yet he heard his mother,
laid his damp hand on hers. He could not speak.
But tears fell from his eyes in sign of love.   1440
The other had breath, and looking toward his sister
and his old mother, Polyneices said:
"Mother, we're dead. I pity you indeed,
and this my sister and my brother corpse,   1445
my friend turned enemy, but still my friend.
Mother, and you, my sister, bury me
in my own land. Persuade the angry state
to grant me this much of my father's soil,
though I got not our house. Close up my eyes,   1450
Mother," he said, and put her hand upon them.
"Farewell, the darkness now is closing in."
So both together breathed out their sad lives.
But their mother, when she looked on this disaster   1455
snatched a sword off the corpses and she did
a dreadful deed. Straight through her neck she drove
the steel. So now she lies among her own.
In death her arms are cast about them both.
Then did the people rush to strife of words,   1460
we claiming that my master won the day,

and they the other. The captains quarreled too.
Some claimed that Polyneices' spear struck first,
the others that dead men have no victory.
Meanwhile, Antigone had left the armies.   1465
They rushed for weapons, but by prudent forethought
the Theban host had halted under arms.
So we fell on them not yet in their armor,
swooping upon the Argive host in haste.
No one withstood us, they fled, and filled the plain.   1470
Blood flowed from myriad corpses slain by spears.
When we had conquered, some set up for Zeus
his trophy-statue, others stripped the corpses
and sent the shields as spoil within the walls.   1475
And others, with Antigone, bring the dead
so their own friends may give them mourning here.
Of these sad contests, some have ended well
for this our city, others ill indeed.

(*Exit the messenger. Enter Antigone with attendants
bearing the bodies of the brothers and Jocasta.*)

Chorus

No longer for hearing alone   1480
is the city's grief. You may see
the three dead on their way
move to the palace, they who found
together their darkened end.

Antigone

No veil now covers the curls on my delicate cheek,   1485
nor in maiden shame have I hidden the blush on my face,
I come as a bacchant, celebrating death.
I have thrown the veil from my hair, my saffron robe hangs loose. 1490
I bring on the dead with my groans.
O Polyneices, you followed your quarreling name.
Woe it was for Thebes; and your strife which was more than
    strife,   1495

but ended as murder on murder has brought the end
of Oedipus' house in blood.
What singer, what singers, O house,   1500
shall I call for this song of grief,
I who bring three kindred bloodily dead,
mother and children, the Fury's delight?
Delight of her who has ruined the house entire,
Oedipus' house; and the ruin began
when he unriddled the riddling song
of the singing Sphinx and slew her dead.   1505

O Father, woe for you!
What Greek or foreign man of a noble race   1510
in the course of our brief day's life
has suffered so many griefs so clear to see?

My poor self, how my song rings out!
What bird that sits in the oak or the high twigs of the olive   1515
will join my lamenting, alone, without my mother,   1520
helping the song of my grief.
Woe for the wailings with which I mourn,
I who shall live my life alone
among my falling tears.

On which of them first shall I cast my shorn-off hair?   1525
On my mother's breasts where I drew my milk,
or the horrible wounds of my brethren?

Oh, oh, come forth from the house,   1530
with your blinded face,
old father Oedipus, show your wretched age,
you who drag out long life
there in the house after casting the dark on your eyes.   1535

(Enter, from the palace, Oedipus.)

Oedipus

Why have you brought me forth to the light,   1540
dragging my blindness along on a stick,

with your pitiful tears, from my bed in the dark,
a gray, invisible ghost of the air, a corpse, a flying dream? 1545

Antigone

You must hear the telling of dreadful news.
Father, your sons are dead.
And so is the wife who tended and guided your stumbling steps,
O Father, woe is me. 1550

Oedipus

Woe for my frightful griefs. One must moan, one must cry aloud.
Three lives gone! My child,
how did they leave the light, what was the fate that fell?

Antigone

Not in reproach do I say it, nor glad at your grief, 1555
but in simple sorrow: the venging power of your curse,
heavy with swords and fire and wicked fightings, fell,
Father, on your sons.

Oedipus

Alas!

Antigone

Why this lament? 1560

Oedipus

My children!

Antigone

You are in grief.
But, Father, if you could see the chariot of the sun
and cast your eyes on these corpses!

Oedipus

It's clear what disaster came on my sons. 1565
But what doom struck down my wife?

Antigone

She showed all men her groaning tears.
She went to her sons as a suppliant, to adjure them by her breast.
Wielding their spears in war with each other,
their mother she found them like lions wild.
There in the flowering meadow, beside Electra's gate,   1570
they were fighting and wounded; already the blood
was running to make them cold.   1575
Hades' libation, which Ares grants.
So taking the bronze-hammered sword from the dead,
she plunged it in flesh, and in grief for her sons,
she fell on her sons.
The god who brought this about
has brought together all of these griefs for our house,   1580
Father, in one short day.

Chorus

This day has started very many sorrows
for Oedipus' house. May later life be better!

Creon

Cease from your mourning. Now it is the time
to think of burial. Oedipus, hear this speech: 1585
Eteocles, your son, gave me the rule
over this land, and made that rule the dowry
for Haemon's marriage with Antigone.
I will not let you live here any more,
for clearly has Teiresias said that never,   1590
while you are here, can the city prosper well.
So, on your way! This proclamation comes
not as an insult, nor am I your enemy.
I simply fear that the Avengers who pursue you
may yet do damage to our fatherland.

Oedipus

O fate, you bred me wretched from the start,　　　　　1595
for suffering, if ever mortal was.
Before I came to light from my mother's womb
Apollo prophesied that I, the unborn,
should kill my father—suffering indeed.
Once I was born, the father who begot me,
counting me as his enemy, tried to kill me　　　　　1600
since he must die through me, and so he sent me,
still a breast-loving baby, to be food
for the wild beasts.
There was I saved. Cithaeron, you should sink
in the depthless chasms of the underworld,　　　　　1605
you who did not destroy me, but your spirit
gave me in servitude to Polybus.
So when, ill-fated, I had killed my father,
I came into my wretched mother's bed
and begot brothers whom I now have killed,　　　　　1610
passing on to my children Laius' curse.
For I am not so foolish in my nature
as to do what I did to my eyes, and to their lives,
if it were not some god who had contrived it.
Well, what's to do now with my wretched self?　　　　1615
Who is to guide the blind man? She who's dead?
Full well I know, were she alive, she would.
Or my good pair of sons? They are no more.
Am I still young enough to make my living?
From what? Creon, why kill me utterly?
For you are killing me if you cast me out.　　　　　1620
Yet I'll not clutch your knees and prove a coward.
Even in misery, I won't betray my birth.

Creon

It is well thought of not to grasp my knees;　　　　　1625
I could not let you live within this land.
Now, of these dead, the one must straight be taken

into the house. The other, he who came
to sack his fatherland with alien help,
that Polyneices do you cast unburied
beyond the boundaries of his fatherland.   1630
And this shall be proclaimed to all the Thebans:
"Whoever lays a wreath upon this corpse
or buries him, shall find reward in death.
Leave him unwept, unburied, food for the birds."
And you, Antigone, leave your triple dirge   1635
and come within the house. For one more day
you shall be maiden, but tomorrow Haemon
and marriage are for you.

Antigone

Father, what wretchedness is on us now!
I mourn for you still more than for the dead.   1640
For yours is not mixed grief heavy and light;
but you are perfect in your misery.
    But you, new ruler, I would ask you this:
Why wrong my father, sending him from the land?
Why lay down laws against this pitiful corpse?   1645

Creon

Eteocles' this decision, and not mine.

Antigone

Senseless. And you a fool to follow it.

Creon

Is it not right to do what is commanded?

Antigone

Not when wrong deeds are wickedly laid down.

Creon

Is it not right to give him to the dogs?   1650

Antigone

 The punishment you seek is not the law's.

Creon

 It is, for a foe who should have been our friend.

Antigone

 Therefore he yielded up his life to fortune.

Creon

 And therefore let him yield his burial.

Antigone

 What wrong, if you should give him his share of earth?   1655

Creon

 Be sure, this man is going to lie unburied.

Antigone

 Then I shall bury him, though the state forbids.

Creon

 Then will you bury yourself close by that corpse.

Antigone

 It's glorious that two friends should lie together.

Creon

 Lay hold on her and take her to the house.   1660

Antigone

 Oh no! I will not loose my hold on him.

Creon

 The gods' these judgments, and not yours, my girl.

Antigone

 And it is not judged right to assault a corpse.

Creon

No one shall lay the damp dust over him.

Antigone

They must. I pray it for Jocasta's sake.   1665

Creon

You work in vain. You cannot get your wish.

Antigone

At least allow me but to bathe his body.

Creon

This too shall be forbidden by the state.

Antigone

But then to bandage up his savage wounds.

Creon

There is no tendance you may give this corpse.   1670

Antigone

O dearest, but at least I kiss your mouth.

Creon

Don't mar your marriage with these lamentations.

Antigone

Do you think that living I will wed your son?

Creon

You'll be forced to it. What refuge from his bed?

Antigone

That night will make me one with the Danaids.   1675

Creon (to Oedipus)

Do you see the daring of her insolence?

Antigone

Let the steel know. My oath is by the sword.

Creon

Why do you wish so to avoid this marriage?

Antigone

I'll go to exile with my wretched father.

Creon

You show nobility, as well as folly.   1680

Antigone

And know you well that I will die with him.

Creon

Go! You'll not kill my son. Now leave the land.

                              (*Exit Creon into the palace.*)

Oedipus

Daughter, I praise your loving zeal for me.

Antigone

How could I marry and send you alone to exile?

Oedipus

Stay and be happy. I will bear my woes.   1685

Antigone

But you are blind. Who'll care for you, my father?

Oedipus

Where fate decides it I will fall and lie.

Antigone

Ah, where is Oedipus and his famous riddle?

Oedipus

Perished. One day, my fortune and my fall.

Antigone

Should I not have some part in all your troubles?   1690

Oedipus

Exile with a blind father is disgrace.

Antigone

Not for the dutiful. Then it is an honor.

Oedipus

Now lead me forward, that I may touch your mother.

Antigone

There. Lay your hand upon your aged dear.

Oedipus

O Mother, O unhappy wife of mine!   1695

Antigone

She lies there piteous, having suffered all.

Oedipus

Where is Eteocles' corpse, and Polyneices'?

Antigone

Here lie they, stretched out close to one another.

Oedipus

Put my unseeing hand upon their faces.

Antigone

There. Lay your hand upon your sons in death.   1700

Oedipus

O dear dead sons, unhappy as your father!

Antigone

    O Polyneices, dearest name to me.

Oedipus

    Now Loxias' doom is working to its end.

Antigone

    What is it? Further woes on top of woes?

Oedipus

    That, wandering, I shall die on Attic soil.   1705

Antigone

    Where? Which of Athens' forts will shelter you?

Oedipus

    It will be Colonus, where the horse-god lives.
    But come, help your blind father on his way,
    since you are eager to be exiled with me.

Antigone

    On to our exile. Father, stretch out your hand.   1710
    I help your steps as the wind helps on the ship.

Oedipus

    I come, I come.
    Oh my poor child, now lead me.

Antigone

    I do, I do, most wretched I,
    of all the girls of Thebes.

Oedipus

    Where shall I set my old foot?   1715
    Daughter, give me my staff.

Antigone

>This way, this way, with me.
>Like this, like this, your feet. 1720
>Your strength is like a dream.

Oedipus

>Oh you, Oh you, who are driving an ancient man
>in exile from his land.
>What terrible things I have suffered! 1725

Antigone

>Why of your suffering speak? Justice regards not the wicked.
>She gives no prizes for folly.

Oedipus

>And I am the one who reached the heights of song.
>When I found out the maiden's riddle, no fool was I. 1730

Antigone

>You go back to the Sphinx, and our shame.
>Stop speaking of past good fortune.
>There awaits you pitiful suffering 1735
>and, somewhere, an exile's death.

>And I leave tears for the girls my friends
>as I part from my fatherland
>to wander, unmaidened.

Oedipus

>Alas for your honest heart! 1740

Antigone

>It will give me fame as great as my father's sorrows.
>I mourn for your wrongs, and for those which are done my
>   brother,
>who goes from the house a corpse to lie unburied.

Father, even if I must die,
in secret I'll bury that body.   1745

Oedipus

Return again to your friends!

Antigone

My own laments are enough.

Oedipus

You can pray to the holy altars.

Antigone

They have had enough of my troubles.   1750

Oedipus

Then go to Bacchus' shrine in the hills
where none but the Maenads are!

Antigone

To go where once I went
in Theban fawnskin clad,
and danced in Semele's holy choir!
It would be no grace I should do the gods.

Oedipus

You that live in my ancestral Thebes, behold this Oedipus,
him who knew the famous riddles and who was a man most
    great.
It was I alone put down the murdering power of the Sphinx.   1760
Now it's I who go dishonored in sad exile from the land.
Yet why do I lament these things and mourn for them in vain?
The constraint the gods lay on us we mortals all must bear.

Chorus

O great Victory, stay with me
all my life.
Nor cease to give me crowns!

THE BACCHAE

Translated by William Arrowsmith

INTRODUCTION TO *THE BACCHAE*

I<small>N</small> 408, at the age of seventy, apparently bitter and broken in spirit, Euripides left Athens for voluntary exile at the court of Archelaus in Macedon; and there, in 406, he died. After his death his three last plays—*The Bacchae, Iphigenia at Aulis*, and the (lost) *Alcmaeon at Corinth*—were brought back to Athens by the dramatist's son, Euripides the Younger, and produced, winning for their dead author the prize so frequently denied him during his lifetime.

Of itself *The Bacchae* needs neither apology nor general introduction. It is, clearly and flatly, that unmistakable thing, a masterpiece; a play which, for dramatic turbulence and comprehensiveness and the sheer power of its poetry, is unmatched by any except the very greatest among ancient and modern tragedies. You have to go to the *Oedipus Tyrannus* or the *Agamemnon* or *Lear* to find anything quite like it in range and power, and even then it remains, of course, unique. But like those plays, *The Bacchae* is finally a mysterious, almost a haunted, work, stalked by divinity and that daemonic power of necessity which for Euripides is the careless source of man's tragic destiny and moral dignity. Elusive, complex and compelling, the play constantly recedes before one's grasp, advancing, not retreating, steadily into deeper chaos and larger order, coming finally to rest only god knows where—which is to say, where it matters.

At the very least then *The Bacchae* requires of its critics gentleness in approaching it and humility in handling; the reader who is not willing to follow where the play, rather than his prejudice, leads him forfeits his quarry. But *sophrosunē* is not a common critical virtue, and despite the critic's clear warning in the fate of Pentheus, the play has suffered more than most from the violence of its interpreters. Perhaps this was only to be expected; because *The Bacchae* is concerned with extreme religious experience, it has naturally engaged the liveliest prejudices of its readers. Thus, apart from the pathologies of criticism, we find a long strain of (peculiarly Christianizing) interpretation which insists, against all probability and the whole experience of the play, that *The Bacchae* is to be understood as a deathbed conversion to the mysteries of Dionysus—Euripides' palinode, as it were, for a lifetime of outspoken hostility to the Olympian system. In revenge, this absurd view was challenged by an even absurder one which, by casting Dionysus as a devil and Pentheus as a noble martyr to human enlightenment, turned the play into a nineteenth-century rationalist tract on the evils of religion. Alternatively, the play has been viewed as a stark schematic conflict between any two of a variety of contrasted abstractions apparently symbolized by Pentheus and Dionysus: reason vs. the irrational; aristocratic skepticism vs. popular piety; civilized order and routine vs. the eruptive force of nature and life. What, in my opinion, vitiates these interpretations is that they are all, or nearly all, incomplete perceptions masking as the whole thing. And like all partial perceptions or half-truths, these are maintained by rejecting whatever in the experience of the play cannot accommodate them; in this way the true power that stalks the play has mostly been expelled or shrouded in a fresh and imposed chaos. Taken in their ensemble, however, these partial perceptions help to round out the whole. For look at the play again and surely what one sees is neither a rationalist tract nor Euripides' dying *confiteor* to Olympus but a play which is moved by profoundly religious feeling and which also happens to display Euripides' familiar hostility to received religion. The inconsistency is only apparent; for in the nature of god as it is defined by the action of the play, the contradictions vanish. Or so I see it. And yet there is more there too.

A few cautions will perhaps be in order. The subject of *The Bacchae* is a (dimly) historical event, the invasion of Hellas by the rites of Dionysus, while the story of Pentheus is Euripides' re-enactment of a myth which doubtlessly embodied Dionysiac ritual.[1] Despite this, *The Bacchae* is neither a study of Dionysiac *cultus* nor a cautionary essay on the effects of religious hysteria; nor, for that matter, however faithfully it may present the *hieros logos* or sacred myth of Dionysiac ritual, is it best read as an anthropological passion-play of the mystical scapegoat or the Year-Daimon. Dionysiac religion is the field on which the action of the play takes place, *not* what

---

[1] The story of Pentheus provided the subject of several ancient tragedies, including a trilogy by Aeschylus.

it is deeply about, and although the play requires a reasonable knowledge about the phenomena of religious ecstasy we call Dionysiac,[2] for the most part it supplies the necessary information and dictates the meaning of its own terms. If we understand that the rewards of the Dionysiac life are here and now, that the frenzied dances of the god are direct manifestations of ecstatic possession, and that the Bacchante, by eating the flesh of the man or animal who temporarily incarnates the god, comes to partake of his divinity, we are in a position to understand the play. One should also perhaps be aware that the view of Dionysiac worship presented by this play is a special one, clearly shaped by the dramatist's needs and modified accordingly; indeed he elaborately warns his fifth-century contemporaries that they must not confound their own experience of Dionysiac worship with that of the play. Thus, for example, against the suspicions of his contemporaries that the Dionysiac mountain-rites were frequently orgiastic in the modern sense of that word, Euripides insists that *his* Bacchae are chaste, and this must be taken as final for the play. Elsewhere he deliberately intrudes anachronism, allowing Teiresias to describe Dionysus pretty much as the fifth century knew his worship: its human sacrifices purged away, its wildness tamed by being fused with Olympian worship and set under state supervision. Beyond this, one should, of course, be aware of the intentional ritual irony that underlies the death of Pentheus—he dies as a scapegoat and a living substitute for the god he rejects. This, however, is an irony of the play, not its meaning, and it is overshadowed by the greatest irony of them all—that this terrible indictment of the anthropomorphic Dionysus that *The Bacchae* makes should have been acted out in the *hieros logos* of the god and presented in the Theater of Dionysus.

Like a number of other Euripidean plays, *The Bacchae* tends to converge about a single central controlling moral term whose meaning is constantly invoked by the action and at the same time altered by it, modified and refreshed under dramatic pressure. This key term is the concept of *sophia* (and its opposite, *amathia*). Constantly

[2] Those interested should consult the Introduction to the Commentary of E. R. Dodds on *The Bacchae* (Oxford, 1944).

thrown up by the action, informing it and guiding it, *sophia* is crucial to the play; but since it is impossible to convey its range of meaning by a single English equivalent, the reader should know what is involved when it occurs. At its broadest, *sophia* is roughly translatable by the English concept of "wisdom"; *sophia*, that is, is primarily a moral rather than an intellectual skill, based upon experience and expressed in significant judgment. But in the Greek—and nowhere more strongly than in the choruses of this play—it implies a firm awareness of one's own nature and therefore of one's place in the scheme of things. In other words, it presupposes self-knowledge, an acceptance of those necessities that compose the limits of human fate; by contrast, the man of *amathia* acts out of a kind of unteachable, ungovernable ignorance of himself and his necessities; he is prone to violence, harshness, and brutality. Thus, in the eyes of the Chorus, Pentheus forfeits any claim to *sophia* because he wantonly, violently, refuses to accept the necessity that Dionysus incarnates: he is, in other words, *amathēs*.

Below the level of this broad sense of *sophia*, however, the range of meaning in the Greek word is extremely wide. For if *sophia* is generically what we mean by wisdom, it is also skill, craft, cleverness, know-how, cunning, smartness, and the specific craft of expedience (in this sense exactly matching one of the commoner uses of the English word "wise"). And so the play exhibits the spectrum of these various *sophiae* classified roughly in terms of the characters, their pretensions and what others think of them. Thus Teiresias possesses the narrow professional *sophia* (i.e., skill, expertise) of the sage and seer, and also shares with Cadmus the more general "wisdom" of ripe old age and long experience. In the Chorus' eyes, Pentheus' *sophia* is that of (mere) cleverness: the quick, articulate, argumentative, shallow cleverness of the trained sophist or "professional intellectual." And finally, lowest of all, there is the knowing animal cunning of the practiced hunter, the cool eye and feline skill of Dionysus stalking his intended victim. Elsewhere the Chorus distinguishes something called *to sophon* which it contrasts unfavorably with high *sophia;* and I think we must understand this to be something like a rubric for the lower *sophiae* or whatever in them contributes to compose the sense of "worldly wisdom," a calculating, shrewd, even opportunistic, skill of the worldly and ambitious, which blinds its possessor to the good that comes—to the Chorus' way of thinking—from acceptance here and now. But over the surface of these meanings of *sophia* the action plays endlessly, testing one *sophia* against another, matching opponents in a steady rage of exposure that in the end inverts all roles and pretensions and leaves the stage, desolate and bleak, to the suffering survivors confronted with the inexorable, pitiless necessity that Dionysus is. We witness, that is, a life and death struggle between rival shapes of *sophia* in the course of which each claimant betrays the thing he stands for: Pentheus' cleverness foundering terribly upon the force he refuses to accept; the *sophia* of the Dionysiac quest nakedly revealed as sheer animal cunning and brutality. We witness, in short, *sophia* becoming *amathia*. There, in *amathia*, the god and his victim meet.

Dramatically, the core of the play is an exquisitely constructed confrontation between the two major opponents, the young god Dionysus and the young man Pentheus. The contrasting itself seems almost schematic: the athletic Pentheus pitted against the languid god; traditional Greek dress contrasted with the outlandish Asiatic livery of the Bacchante; the angry, impetuous, heavy-handed young man as against the smiling, soft-spoken, feline effortlessness of Dionysus; the self-ignorant man confronted with the humanized shape of his necessity. Below the contrasts run the resemblances, for these young rivals, we need to remember, are first cousins and they share a family likeness. Thus each is deeply jealous of his own *personal* honor and ruthless in enmity; each is intolerant of opposition to his will. The god, of course, in the end prevails, but the drama of the god's gradual usurpation of his victim depends for its effectiveness and irony upon our understanding of the initial confrontation. For it is by playing upon Pentheus' vulnerability, his deep ignorance of his own nature, that the god is able to possess him, humiliate him and finally to destroy him. For Dionysus, the motives of humiliation and revenge are crucial; and Dionysus is a supreme artist in exact poetic vengeance. Thus, point for point, each of Pentheus' threats, insults, and outrages is revenged with ironic and ferocious precision as Pentheus goes off, waving his thyrsus, tricked out in woman's robes and a fawn-skin, to his death on the mountain as the sacrificial surrogate of the god. We see in his costume and madness not merely his complete humiliation but the total loss of identity the change implies. And so the reversal is complete, the hunter become the hunted and the hunted the hunter.

If we consider Pentheus in isolation, it should be immediately apparent that his is not the stuff of which tragic heroes are made. Nor, for that matter, is he a convincing candidate to symbolize rea son against the Dionysiac irrational. He is, in fact, a deeply unreasonable man, intemperate in anger and utterly unconvinced by reasonable evidence. Around him cluster almost all the harsh words of the Greek moral vocabulary: he is violent, stubborn, self-willed, arbitrary, impatient of tradition and custom, impious, unruly, and immoderate. At times he evinces the traits of a stock tragedy-tyrant, loud with threats and bluster, prone to confuse the meaning of subject with slave. But so, I think, he must be shown in order to be presented for what he is: ignorant of himself and his nature, profoundly *amathēs*. Yet as he makes his entrance, breathing fury against the Maenads, I think we are meant to be struck by his extreme youth. Just how old he is, Euripides does not tell us; but since he is presented as still a beardless boy at the time of his death (see ll. 1185 ff.), he cannot very well be much more than sixteen or seventeen. And this youth seems to me dramatically important, helping to qualify Pentheus' prurient sexual imagination (for the voyeurism which in a grown man would be overtly pathological is at most an obsessive and morbid curiosity in a boy) and later serving to enlist our sympathies sharply on the side of the boy-victim of a ruthless god. Pentheus' *hybris*, of course, remains, for ignorance of one's identity and necessities is finally no excuse. And yet, in the Greek view of things, extreme youth should help to extenuate the offense. For the young are naturally susceptible to *hybris*, that simple overflow of the dangerous pride (or the suppressed strength) of the flesh and spirit into outrage and violence; and, being susceptible, they merit both understanding and lenience. *Sophia*, after all, is not a young man's virtue, and though necessity may be inflexible, our humanity is not. How-

ever much Pentheus' conduct may outrage sympathy, his youth and
utter human helplessness before the awful shape of his necessity are
addressed directly to our understanding and compassion.

But Pentheus is something more than a mere personification of
suppressed necessity, and his *hybris* has social as well as sexual roots.
At least it seems to me that Euripides has taken elaborate pains to
show in Pentheus the proud iconoclastic innovator, rebelling
against tradition, outside of the community's *nomos* (custom as law),
and disdainful of any power above man. Ranged against him are
Cadmus, Teiresias, and the Chorus, who all alike appeal to the massive authority of tradition and folk-belief and constantly invoke
against the scoffer the full force of *dikē* (custom incarnate as justice)
and *sophrosunē* (very roughly, humility). Thus in flat ominous opposition to Pentheus' lonely arrogance of the "exceptional" (*perissos*)
individual, superior and contemptuous, defying the community's
nomos in the name of his own self-will, is set the chorus' tyrannous
tradition: "Beyond the old beliefs, no thought, no act shall go" (ll.
891–92). We have, that is, a head-on collision between those who,
for all their piety, represent the full-blown tyranny of popular custom and conforming tradition and the arrogant exemplar of the
ruthlessly antitraditional mind. Both sides are alike in the cruel and
bigoted violence with which they meet opposition and the *sophrosunē* and *dikē* and *sophia* which they variously claim mock their per-
tensions and implicitly condemn their conduct. If in the end the
conduct of the Chorus and Dionysus outrage our sympathies and
enlist them on Pentheus' behalf, it is because, in the nature of things,
the *amathia* of a man is less heinous than that of a god. But both are
amatheis, Pentheus and Dionysus alike. Beyond this point certainty
is impossible. But I suspect that the play employs Dionysus and
Pentheus and the conflict between them as a bitter image of Athens
and Hellas terribly divided between the forces that, for Euripides,
more than anything else destroyed them: on the one side, the con-
servative tradition in its extreme corruption, disguising avarice for
power with the fair professions of the traditional *aretai*, meeting all
opposition with the terrible tyranny of popular piety, and disclosing
in its actions the callousness and refined cruelty of civilized barba-

rism; on the other side, the exceptional individual, selfish and ego-
tistical, impatient of tradition and public welfare alike, stubborn,
demagogic, and equally brutal in action. This interpretation, however, should not be pressed; if it is there at all, it is tenuously, sugges-
tively there, informing the terms of a social conflict between Pentheus and Dionysus' followers which is otherwise unexplained.

Dionysus himself is a difficult figure only, I think, because he is
so clearly a transitional one, a figure which under dramatic pressure
is in the process of becoming something quite different from what he
was at the outset. What the divinity of Dionysus represents, however, should be clear enough from the play: the incarnate life-force
itself, the uncontrollable chaotic eruption of nature in individuals
and cities; the thrust of the sap in the tree and the blood in the veins,
the "force that through the green fuse drives the flower." As such,
he is amoral, neither good nor bad, a necessity capable of blessing
those who (like the Asian Bacchantes) accept him, and of destroying or maddening those who (like Pentheus) deny him. Like any
necessity, he is ambiguous, raw power: his *thyrsus* spurts honey for
the bands of the blessed but becomes a killing weapon when turned
against the scoffer. But to the question, Is Dionysus a traditional
"Olympian" deity or is he the amoral and daemonic personification
of the force he represents? the answer, I think, is clearly that he is,
at different times, both. If he begins the play as a conventional, anthropomorphic deity of the Homeric type, endowed with human
virtues and human passions, he undergoes a progress which more
and more forces him into the shape of the amoral necessity he represents and which culminates in his final epiphany as a pitiless, daemonic, necessitous power. In the withering of his traditional *sophia*
through the dramatic demonstration that his only *sophia* is the cunning of the hunter, his traditional divinity also withers. For divinity
divested of morality becomes daemonic (not devilish but the reality
of awful, inscrutable, careless power), like Dionysus here. Just so, in
the *Hippolytus*, we can see coming into focus beneath the lineaments
of the Olympian Aphrodite the inexorable, amoral face of the nar-
rowly sexual necessity of man and nature. It needs, however, to be
insisted that these personified necessities of the Euripidean stage are

not mere naturalistic psychological symbols. They are precisely *daimones*, the great powers that stalk the world, real with a terrible reality, the source of man's very condition, the necessities which determine his life. And if the feelings stirred by what is limited before the unlimited are religious, then man's attitude toward these *daimones* is religious, the veneration and awe the fated must feel before the great gods of existence: Death, Life, Sex, Grief, Joy. *Sophia* accepts because it is a wisdom of experience, based on awe learned of both joy and bitter suffering.

Grouped about Dionysus and Pentheus, variously informing their struggle or suffering its consequences, stand the other characters of the play—Teiresias, Cadmus, Agave, and the Chorus of Asian Bacchantes. Of these Agave has been put here almost entirely to suffer, and the very extremity and brutality of what she suffers is unmistakably intended to expose the brutal ferocity of Dionysus. For it is in her person and through her words as she moves from the terrible irony of her triumphal entrance to one of the cruelest (and finest) recognition scenes in tragedy that the balance of sympathies shifts decisively against Dionysus, exposing him for what he is; *this*, she cries ecstatically, holding up the head of her dismembered son, is the quarry of the chase, the great Dionysiac hunt for "those great, those manifest, those certain goals, achieving which our lives are blest." Where Pentheus' passion ends, hers begins, even more terrible than his, driving us relentlessly on to the true epiphany of the god. What god, we want to know, no matter what provocation, could make a mother dismember her son and still retain his *sophia*? And the answer, of course, is: no god but necessity, which is not wise and, though divine, has no altars.

Teiresias and Cadmus, however, are more problematic. Each, as we have seen, claims a distinctive *sophia* and yet they fail to convince us. In part, this is due to the deliberate pathos and incongruity of their entrance: two doddering old men in fawn-skins off to the dances on the mountain. But although they hover on the edge of comedy, they are not funny but pathetic: two incongruous, shrewd old mummers of ecstasy. For they are not, we soon discover, among the number of those who dance in the sheer conviction of delight, their bodies possessed and compelled by the inward god—though they would like to convince both us and each other that they are so possessed. They dance in shrewd expedience, Cadmus realistically aware of the value of having a god in the family, Teiresias sensing the future greatness of the new religion and the opportunities for priestly expertise. Piously, self-righteously, they go through the motions of accepting their necessity; but if elated at first by their role and costume, they make their exit in a state of near exhaustion, propping each other up and limping off, a long way from ecstasy. And there is irony again, of course, when Teiresias, affecting the role of staunch traditionalist, lectures Pentheus on the nature of Dionysus with the pedantic etymologizing zeal of a professional sophist. But their function here is to occupy the mean of worldly wisdom (*to sophon*) between the *sophia* claimed by the Chorus and the *amathia* of Pentheus. They are trimmers and compromisers, true men of the mean, set in sharp contrast to Pentheus, who, contemptuous of any compromise, temperamentally inhabits extreme positions. As such they round out the range of attitudes which center on Dionysus: the utter possessed madness of the Theban women on the mountain which is typified by Agave; the calmer, more reflective worship of the Chorus of Asian Bacchae; the worldly compromising temper of the two old men, and the passionate and sweeping denial of the god by Pentheus.

The Chorus here deserves mention also, all the more since its role as Bacchante has necessarily been modified by its choral and dramatic functions. For it is from their lips—impressively confirmed and amplified by the two messengers—that we get what is so crucial to the play, the full poetic resonance of the Dionysiac life; in the sweep and beauty of their language we are meant to feel what Dionysus means for suffering mortality, the direct eruption of deity in blessing and miracle. Dionysus, as we have seen, is ambivalent: "most terrible, and yet most gentle, to mankind." The exodus of the play emphasizes the terrible aspect of the god, and so it is important for dramatic balance that the gentle side of Dionysus be given the fullest possible statement. Moreover, we can believe the Chorus, for, unlike the Maenads on the mountain, the Bacchantes of the Chorus are not possessed. A divinity, true, moves in their words, but less as a chaotic wildness than as a controlled and passionate conviction. Indeed, at times these foreign women seem to be surprisingly Hellenized and their sentiments indistinguishable from those of a standard tragic chorus. They tend to alternate, that is, between a feverish (Asiatic) hymning of the god and slow, reflective, traditional (Greek) gnomes on the nature of divinity and the dangers of disobedience. This duality *may* derive from their double role as dramatic Chorus and followers of Dionysus, or it may be that Euripides is anxious to set before us an image of that controlled Dionysiac experience with which the fifth century was familiar. For by means of this anachronism, he can, without deeply violating dramatic consistency, show the point at which the convinced (but not possessed) Bacchante can separate her humanity from the god. Just this, of course, takes place at the end of the play, and its importance should not be minimized. For, despite their having danced for joy at the death of Pentheus, the Chorus, when finally confronted by Agave bearing Pentheus' head on her *thyrsus*, is moved to unmistakable horror and pity. In their feelings, they clearly separate themselves from the god with whom they have hitherto identified themselves completely. Bacchantes they may be, the scene seems to say, but they are human first. Against Dionysus who shows himself utterly inflexible and ruthless to the end, their reaction is decisive. And the tone of pity sets the stage for the all-important exodus.

For what we see in the exodus is, I think, the discovery of compassion, and in this the exodus of *The Bacchae* follows good Euripidean precedent. One thinks of the *Hippolytus* (so much like *The Bacchae* in so many ways) where, under the yoke of another inflexible necessity, compassion and understanding flower between Theseus and the dying Hippolytus; or of *Heracles* and the same discovery of love and need between the anguished hero and his friend and his father in the face of the bleak necessity of a careless, ruthless heaven. So here, beneath the inexorable harshness of that necessity called Dionysus, out of their anguish and suffering, Agave and Cadmus discover compassion, the pity that is born from shared suffering. In this they declare their humanity and a moral dignity which heaven, lacking those limits which make men suffer *into* dignity and compassion, can never understand or equal. This is their moral victory, the only victory the doomed can claim over the necessities which make them suffer. But it is a great victory; for by accepting their necessities in anguish, they claim the uniquely human skill of *sophia*, the acceptance of necessity and doom which teaches compassion.[3] It is that faith and that fate which, in Euripides, makes man human, not mere god.

The text of my translation is the Oxford text of Gilbert Murray, supplemented by the brilliant commentary of E. R. Dodds.

[3] Cf. Euripides' *Electra*, ll. 294–95, where Orestes states that pity (*to oiktos*) is never found among the *amatheis* but only among the wise (*sophoisi*).

CHARACTERS

Dionysus (also called Bromius, Evius, and Bacchus)

Chorus of Asian Bacchae (followers of Dionysus)

Teiresias

Cadmus

Pentheus

Attendant

First Messenger

Second Messenger

Agave

Coryphaeus (chorus leader)

For Anne and George
ex voto
XAIPETE

THE BACCHAE

SCENE: *Before the royal palace at Thebes. On the left is the way to Cithaeron; on the right, to the city. In the center of the orchestra stands, still smoking, the vine-covered tomb of Semele, mother of Dionysus.*

Enter Dionysus. He is of soft, even effeminate, appearance. His face is beardless; he is dressed in a fawn-skin and carries a thyrsus (i.e., a stalk of fennel tipped with ivy leaves). On his head he wears a wreath of ivy, and his long blond curls ripple down over his shoulders. Throughout the play he wears a smiling mask.

Dionysus

I am Dionysus, the son of Zeus,
come back to Thebes, this land where I was born.
My mother was Cadmus' daughter, Semele by name,
midwived by fire, delivered by the lightning's
blast.

    And here I stand, a god incognito,
disguised as man, beside the stream of Dirce   5
and the waters of Ismenus. There before the palace
I see my lightning-married mother's grave,
and there upon the ruins of her shattered house
the living fire of Zeus still smolders on
in deathless witness of Hera's violence and rage
against my mother. But Cadmus wins my praise: 10
he has made this tomb a shrine, sacred to my mother.
It was I who screened her grave with the green
of the clustering vine.

               Far behind me lie
those golden-rivered lands, Lydia and Phrygia,
where my journeying began. Overland I went,
across the steppes of Persia where the sun strikes hotly
down, through Bactrian fastness and the grim waste   15
of Media. Thence to rich Arabia I came;

and so, along all Asia's swarming littoral
of towered cities where Greeks and foreign nations,
mingling, live, my progress made. There
I taught my dances to the feet of living men,
establishing my mysteries and rites
that I might be revealed on earth for what I am:
a god.

        And thence to Thebes.

                This city, first   20
in Hellas, now shrills and echoes to my women's cries,
their ecstasy of joy. Here in Thebes
I bound the fawn-skin to the women's flesh and armed
their hands with shafts of ivy. For I have come   25
to refute that slander spoken by my mother's sisters—
those who least had right to slander her.
They said that Dionysus was no son of Zeus,
but Semele had slept beside a man in love
and fathered off her shame on Zeus—a fraud, they sneered,   30
contrived by Cadmus to protect his daughter's name.
They said she lied, and Zeus in anger at that lie
blasted her with lightning.

                Because of that offense
I have stung them with frenzy, hounded them from home
up to the mountains where they wander, crazed of mind,
and compelled to wear my orgies' livery.
Every woman in Thebes—but the women only—   35
I drove from home, mad. There they sit,
rich and poor alike, even the daughters of Cadmus,
beneath the silver firs on the roofless rocks.
Like it or not, this city must learn its lesson:
it lacks initiation in my mysteries;   40
that I shall vindicate my mother Semele
and stand revealed to mortal eyes as the god
she bore to Zeus.

           Cadmus the king has abdicated,
leaving his throne and power to his grandson Pentheus;

who now revolts against divinity, in *me;*   45
thrusts *me* from his offerings; forgets *my* name
in his prayers. Therefore I shall *prove* to him
and every man in Thebes that I am god
indeed. And when my worship is established here,
and all is well, then I shall go my way
and be revealed to other men in other lands.   50
But if the men of Thebes attempt to force
my Bacchae from the mountainside by threat of arms,
I shall marshal my Maenads and take the field.
To these ends I have laid my deity aside
and go disguised as man.

> *(He wheels and calls offstage.)*

            On, my women,   55
women who worship me, women whom I led
out of Asia where Tmolus heaves its rampart
over Lydia!
            On, comrades of my progress here!
Come, and with your native Phrygian drum—
Rhea's drum and mine—pound at the palace doors   60
of Pentheus! Let the city of Thebes behold you,
while I return among Cithaeron's forest glens
where my Bacchae wait and join their whirling dances.

> *(Exit Dionysus as the Chorus of Asian Bacchae comes
> dancing in from the right. They are dressed in
> fawn-skins, crowned with ivy, and carry
> thyrsi, timbrels, and flutes.)*

Chorus

    Out of the land of Asia,
    down from holy Tmolus,   65
    speeding the service of god,
    for Bromius we come!
    Hard are the labors of god;
    hard, but his service is sweet.
    Sweet to serve, sweet to cry:
                Bacchus!   Evohé!

—You on the streets!
                    —You on the roads!
                                        —Make way!
—Let every mouth be hushed. Let no ill-omened words   70
   profane your tongues.
                        —Make way! Fall back!
                                              —Hush.
—For now I raise the old, old hymn to Dionysus.

—Blessèd, blessèd are those who know the mysteries of god.
—Blessèd is he who hallows his life in the worship of god,
      he whom the spirit of god possesseth, who is one
      with those who belong to the holy body of god.   75
—Blessèd are the dancers and those who are purified,
      who dance on the hill in the holy dance of god.
—Blessèd are they who keep the rite of Cybele the Mother.
—Blessèd are the thyrsus-bearers, those who wield in their hands
      the holy wand of god.   80
—Blessèd are those who wear the crown of the ivy of god.
—Blessèd, blessèd are they: Dionysus is their god!

—On, Bacchae, on, you Bacchae,
      bear your god in triumph home!
      Bear on the god, son of god,
      escort your Dionysus home!   85
      Bear him down from Phrygian hill,
      attend him through the streets of Hellas!

—So his mother bore him once
      in labor bitter; lightning-struck,
      forced by fire that flared from Zeus,   90
      consumed, she died, untimely torn,
      in childbed dead by blow of light!
      Of light the son was born!

—Zeus it was who saved his son;   95
      with speed outrunning mortal eye,

bore him to a private place,
bound the boy with clasps of gold;
in his thigh as in a womb,
concealed his son from Hera's eyes.

—And when the weaving Fates fulfilled the time,   100
the bull-horned god was born of Zeus. In joy
he crowned his son, set serpents on his head—
wherefrom, in piety, descends to us
the Maenad's writhing crown, her *chevelure* of snakes.

—O Thebes, nurse of Semele,   105
crown your hair with ivy!
Grow green with bryony!
Redden with berries! O city,
with boughs of oak and fir,   110
come dance the dance of god!
Fringe your skins of dappled fawn
with tufts of twisted wool!
Handle with holy care
the violent wand of god!
And let the dance begin!
He is Bromius who runs   115
to the mountain!
                    to the mountain!
where the throng of women waits,
driven from shuttle and loom,
possessed by Dionysus!

—And I praise the holies of Crete,   120
the caves of the dancing Curetes,
there where Zeus was born,
where helmed in triple tier
around the primal drum
the Corybantes danced. They,   125
they were the first of all
whose whirling feet kept time

to the strict beat of the taut hide
and the squeal of the wailing flute.
Then from them to Rhea's hands
the holy drum was handed down;
but, stolen by the raving Satyrs,   130
fell at last to me and now
accompanies the dance
which every other year
celebrates your name:
    Dionysus!

—He is sweet upon the mountains. He drops to the earth   135
    from the running packs.
He wears the holy fawn-skin. He hunts the wild goat
    and kills it.
He delights in the raw flesh.
He runs to the mountains of Phrygia, to the mountains
    of Lydia he runs!   140
He is Bromius who leads us! *Evohé!*

— With milk the earth flows! It flows with wine!
It runs with the nectar of bees!

—Like frankincense in its fragrance
is the blaze of the torch he bears.   145
Flames float out from his trailing wand
    as he runs, as he dances,
    kindling the stragglers,
    spurring with cries,
and his long curls stream to the wind!   150

—And he cries, as they cry, *Evohé!*—
    On, Bacchae!
    On, Bacchae!
Follow, glory of golden Tmolus,
    hymning god   155
    with a rumble of drums,

with a cry, *Evohé!* to the Evian god,
with a cry of Phrygian cries,
when the holy flute like honey plays   160
the sacred song of those who go
to the mountain!
                    to the mountain!   165

—Then, in ecstasy, like a colt by its grazing mother,
the Bacchante runs with flying feet, she leaps!

> (*The Chorus remains grouped in two semicircles about the
> orchestra as Teiresias makes his entrance. He is in-
> congruously dressed in the bacchant's fawn-skin
> and is crowned with ivy. Old and blind,
> he uses his thyrsus to tap his way.*)

Teiresias

Ho there, who keeps the gates?
                         Summon Cadmus—   170
Cadmus, Agenor's son, the stranger from Sidon
who built the towers of our Thebes.
                         Go, someone.
Say Teiresias wants him. He will know what errand
brings me, that agreement, age with age, we made   175
to deck our wands, to dress in skins of fawn
and crown our heads with ivy.

> (*Enter Cadmus from the palace. Dressed in Dionysiac
> costume and bent almost double with age, he is an
> incongruous and pathetic figure.*)

Cadmus
                         My old friend,
I knew it must be you when I heard your summons.
For there's a wisdom in his voice that makes
the man of wisdom known.
                         But here I am,
dressed in the costume of the god, prepared to go.   180
Insofar as we are able, Teiresias, we must

do honor to this god, for he was born
my daughter's son, who has been revealed to men,
the god, Dionysus.
                  Where shall we go, where
shall we tread the dance, tossing our white heads
in the dances of god?
                  Expound to me, Teiresias.   185
For in such matters you are wise.
                  Surely
I could dance night and day, untiringly
beating the earth with my thyrsus! And how sweet it is
to forget my old age.

Teiresias

                  It is the same with me.
I too feel young, young enough to dance.   190

Cadmus

Good. Shall we take our chariots to the mountain?

Teiresias

Walking would be better. It shows more honor
to the god.

Cadmus

                  So be it. I shall lead, my old age
conducting yours.

Teiresias

                  The god will guide us there
with no effort on our part.

Cadmus

                  Are we the only men   195
who will dance for Bacchus?

Teiresias

                  They are all blind.
Only we can see.

Cadmus

> But we delay too long.
> Here, take my arm.

Teiresias

> Link my hand in yours.

Cadmus

> I am a man, nothing more. I do not scoff
> at heaven.

Teiresias

> We do not trifle with divinity.   200
> No, we are the heirs of customs and traditions
> hallowed by age and handed down to us
> by our fathers. No quibbling logic can topple *them*,
> whatever subtleties this clever age invents.
> People may say: "Aren't you ashamed? At your age,
> going dancing, wreathing your head with ivy?"   205
> Well, I am *not* ashamed. Did the god declare
> that just the young or just the old should dance?
> No, he desires his honor from all mankind.
> He wants no one excluded from his worship.

Cadmus

> Because you cannot see, Teiresias, let me be   210
> interpreter for you this once. Here comes
> the man to whom I left my throne, Echion's son,
> Pentheus, hastening toward the palace. He seems
> excited and disturbed. Yes, listen to him.

> > (Enter Pentheus from the right. He is a young man of
> > athletic build, dressed in traditional Greek dress;
> > like Dionysus, he is beardless. He enters
> > excitedly, talking to the attendants
> > who accompany him.)

Pentheus

> I happened to be away, out of the city,   215
> but reports reached me of some strange mischief here,

stories of our women leaving home to frisk
in mock ecstasies among the thickets on the mountain,
dancing in honor of the latest divinity,
a certain Dionysus, whoever he may be!   220
In their midst stand bowls brimming with wine.
And then, one by one, the women wander off
to hidden nooks where they serve the lusts of men.
Priestesses of Bacchus they claim they are,
but it's really Aphrodite they adore.   225
I have captured some of them; my jailers
have locked them away in the safety of our prison.
Those who run at large shall be hunted down
out of the mountains like the animals they are—
yes, my own mother Agave, and Ino
and Autonoë, the mother of Actaeon.   230
In no time at all I shall have them trapped
in iron nets and stop this obscene disorder.

    I am also told a foreigner has come to Thebes
from Lydia, one of those charlatan magicians,
with long yellow curls smelling of perfumes,   235
with flushed cheeks and the spells of Aphrodite
in his eyes. His days and nights he spends
with women and girls, dangling before them the joys
of initiation in his mysteries.
But let me bring him underneath that roof
and I'll stop his pounding with his wand and tossing   240
his head. By god, I'll have his head cut off!
And *this* is the man who claims that Dionysus
is a god and was sewn into the thigh of Zeus,
when, in point of fact, that same blast of lightning
consumed him and his mother both for her lie   245
that she had lain with Zeus in love. Whoever
this stranger is, aren't such impostures,
such unruliness, worthy of hanging?

                    (*For the first time he sees Teiresias and
                      Cadmus in their Dionysiac costumes.*)

What!

But this is incredible! Teiresias the seer
tricked out in a dappled fawn-skin!

          And *you,*
you, my own grandfather, playing at the bacchant   250
with a wand!

            Sir, I shrink to see your old age
so foolish. Shake that ivy off, grandfather!
Now drop that wand. Drop it, I say.

                  (He wheels on Teiresias.)

          Aha,
I see: this is *your* doing, Teiresias.   255
Yes, you want still another god revealed to men
so you can pocket the profits from burnt offerings
and bird-watching. By heaven, only your age
restrains me now from sending you to prison
with those Bacchic women for importing here to Thebes
these filthy mysteries. When once you see   260
the glint of wine shining at the feasts of women,
then you may be sure the festival is rotten.

Coryphaeus

What blasphemy! Stranger, have you no respect
for heaven? For Cadmus who sowed the dragon teeth?
Will the son of Echion disgrace his house?   265

Teiresias

Give a wise man an honest brief to plead
and his eloquence is no remarkable achievement.
But you are glib; your phrases come rolling out
smoothly on the tongue, as though your words were wise
instead of foolish. The man whose glibness flows
from his conceit of speech declares the thing he is: 270
a worthless and a stupid citizen.

            I tell you,
this god whom you ridicule shall someday have

enormous power and prestige throughout Hellas.
Mankind, young man, possesses two supreme blessings.
First of these is the goddess Demeter, or Earth— 275
whichever name you choose to call her by.
It was she who gave to man his nourishment of grain.
But after her there came the son of Semele,
who matched her present by inventing liquid wine
as his gift to man. For filled with that good gift,
suffering mankind forgets its grief; from it 280
comes sleep; with it oblivion of the troubles
of the day. There is no other medicine
for misery. And when we pour libations
to the gods, we pour the god of wine himself
that through his intercession man may win 285
the favor of heaven.

         You sneer, do you, at that story
that Dionysus was sewed into the thigh of Zeus?
Let me teach you what that really means. When Zeus
rescued from the thunderbolt his infant son,
he brought him to Olympus. Hera, however,
plotted at heart to hurl the child from heaven. 290
Like the god he is, Zeus countered her. Breaking off
a tiny fragment of that ether which surrounds the world,
he molded from it a dummy Dionysus.
This he *showed* to Hera, but with time men garbled
the word and said that Dionysus had been *sewed* 295
into the thigh of Zeus. This was their story,
whereas, in fact, Zeus *showed* the dummy to Hera
and gave it as a hostage for his son.

                     Moreover,
this is a god of prophecy. His worshippers,
like madmen, are endowed with mantic powers.
For when the god enters the body of a man 300
he fills him with the breath of prophecy.

                  Besides,

he has usurped even the functions of warlike Ares.
Thus, at times, you see an army mustered under arms
stricken with panic before it lifts a spear.
This panic comes from Dionysus.

                   Someday   305
you shall even see him bounding with his torches
among the crags at Delphi, leaping the pastures
that stretch between the peaks, whirling and waving
his thyrsus: great throughout Hellas.

                      Mark my words,
Pentheus. Do not be so certain that power   310
is what matters in the life of man; do not mistake
for wisdom the fantasies of your sick mind.
Welcome the god to Thebes; crown your head;
pour him libations and join his revels.

    Dionysus does not, I admit, *compel* a woman
to be chaste. Always and in every case   315
it is her character and nature that keeps
a woman chaste. But even in the rites of Dionysus,
the chaste woman will not be corrupted.

                     Think:
you are pleased when men stand outside your doors
and the city glorifies the name of Pentheus.   320
And so the god: he too delights in glory.
But Cadmus and I, whom you ridicule, will crown
our heads with ivy and join the dances of the god—
an ancient foolish pair perhaps, but dance
we must. Nothing you have said would make me
change my mind or flout the will of heaven.   325
You are mad, grievously mad, beyond the power
of any drugs to cure, for you are drugged
with madness.

Coryphaeus
             Apollo would approve your words.
Wisely you honor Bromius: a great god.

Cadmus

My boy,

Teiresias advises well. Your home is here   330
with us, with our customs and traditions, not
outside, alone. Your mind is distracted now,
and what you think is sheer delirium.
Even if this Dionysus is no god,
as you assert, persuade yourself that he is.
The fiction is a noble one, for Semele will seem   335
to be the mother of a god, and this confers
no small distinction on our family.

You saw

that dreadful death your cousin Actaeon died
when those man-eating hounds he had raised himself
savaged him and tore his body limb from limb
because he boasted that his prowess in the hunt surpassed   340
the skill of Artemis.

Do not let his fate be yours.

Here, let me wreathe your head with leaves of ivy.
Then come with us and glorify the god.

Pentheus

Take your hands off me! Go worship your Bacchus,
but do not wipe your madness off on me.
By god, I'll make him pay, the man who taught you   345
this folly of yours.

(He turns to his attendants.)

Go, someone, this instant,

to the place where this prophet prophesies.
Pry it up with crowbars, heave it over,
upside down; demolish everything you see.
Throw his fillets out to wind and weather.   350
That will provoke him more than anything.
As for the rest of you, go and scour the city
for that effeminate stranger, the man who infects our women
with this strange disease and pollutes our beds.

And when you take him, clap him in chains   355
and march him here. He shall die as he deserves—
by being stoned to death. He shall come to rue
his merrymaking here in Thebes.

(Exeunt attendants.)

Teiresias

Reckless fool,

you do not know the consequences of your words.
You talked madness before, but this is raving
lunacy!

Cadmus, let us go and pray   360

for this raving fool and for this city too,
pray to the god that no awful vengeance strike
from heaven.

Take your staff and follow me.

Support me with your hands, and I shall help you too
lest we stumble and fall, a sight of shame,
two old men together.

But go we must,   365

acknowledging the service that we owe to god,
Bacchus, the son of Zeus.

And yet take care

lest someday your house repent of Pentheus
in its sufferings. I speak not prophecy
but fact. The words of fools finish in folly.

(Exeunt Teiresias and Cadmus. Pentheus
retires into the palace.)

Chorus

—Holiness, queen of heaven,   370
  Holiness on golden wing
  who hover over earth,
  do you hear what Pentheus says?
  Do you hear his blasphemy
  against the prince of the blessèd,   375
  the god of garlands and banquets,

Bromius, Semele's son?
These blessings he gave:
laughter to the flute 380
and the loosing of cares
when the shining wine is spilled
at the feast of the gods,
and the wine-bowl casts its sleep 385
on feasters crowned with ivy.

—A tongue without reins,
defiance, unwisdom—
their end is disaster.
But the life of quiet good,
the wisdom that accepts— 390
these abide unshaken,
preserving, sustaining
the houses of men.
Far in the air of heaven,
the sons of heaven live.
But they watch the lives of men.
And what passes for wisdom is not; 395
unwise are those who aspire,
who outrange the limits of man.
Briefly, we live. Briefly,
then die. Wherefore, I say,
he who hunts a glory, he who tracks
some boundless, superhuman dream,
may lose his harvest here and now
and garner death. Such men are mad, 400
   their counsels evil.

—O let me come to Cyprus,
island of Aphrodite,
homes of the loves that cast
their spells on the hearts of men!
Or Paphos where the hundred- 405
mouthed barbarian river

« 170 »

brings ripeness without rain!
To Pieria, haunt of the Muses, 410
and the holy hill of Olympus!
O Bromius, leader, god of joy,
Bromius, take me there!
There the lovely Graces go,
and there Desire, and there
the right is mine to worship 415
 as I please.

—The deity, the son of Zeus,
in feast, in festival, delights.
He loves the goddess Peace,
generous of good,
preserver of the young. 420
To rich and poor he gives
the simple gift of wine,
the gladness of the grape.
 But him who scoffs he hates,
and him who mocks his life,
the happiness of those
for whom the day is blessed 425
but doubly blessed the night;
whose simple wisdom shuns the thoughts
of proud, uncommon men and all
their god-encroaching dreams.
But what the common people do, 430
the things that simple men believe,
 I too believe and do.

> (*As Penthus reappears from the palace,*
> *enter from the left several attendants*
> *leading Dionysus captive.*)

Attendant

Pentheus, here we are; not empty-handed either.
We captured the quarry you sent us out to catch. 435
But our prey here was tame: refused to run

or hide, held out his hands as willing as you please,
completely unafraid. His ruddy cheeks were flushed
as though with wine, and he stood there smiling,
making no objection when we roped his hands   440
and marched him here. It made me feel ashamed.
"Listen, stranger," I said, "I am not to blame.
We act under orders from Pentheus. He ordered
your arrest."

     As for those women you clapped in chains
and sent to the dungeon, they're gone, clean away,   445
went skipping off to the fields crying on their god
Bromius. The chains on their legs snapped apart
by themselves. Untouched by any human hand,
the doors swung wide, opening of their own accord.
Sir, this stranger who has come to Thebes is full   450
of many miracles. I know no more than that.
The rest is your affair.

Pentheus

     Untie his hands.
We have him in our net. He may be quick,
but he cannot escape us now, I think.

    (While the servants untie Dionysus' hands, Pentheus
      attentively scrutinizes his prisoner. Then
      the servants step back, leaving Pentheus
      and Dionysus face to face.)

        So,
you *are* attractive, stranger, at least to women—
which explains, I think, your presence here in Thebes.
Your curls are long. You do not wrestle, I take it.   455
And what fair skin you have—you must take care of it—
no daylight complexion; no, it comes from the night
when you hunt Aphrodite with your beauty.

         Now then,
who are you and from where?

Dionysus

It is nothing   460
to boast of and easily told. You have heard, I suppose,
of Mount Tmolus and her flowers?

Pentheus

I know the place.
It rings the city of Sardis.

Dionysus

I come from there.
My country is Lydia.

Pentheus

Who is this god whose worship
you have imported into Hellas?

Dionysus

Dionysus, the son of Zeus.   465
He initiated me.

Pentheus

You have some local Zeus
who spawns new gods?

Dionysus

He is the same as yours—
the Zeus who married Semele.

Pentheus

How did you see him?
In a dream or face to face?

Dionysus

Face to face.
He gave me his rites.

Pentheus

What form do they take,   470
these mysteries of yours?

Dionysus

It is forbidden
to tell the uninitiate.

Pentheus

Tell me the benefits
that those who know your mysteries enjoy.

Dionysus

I am forbidden to say. But they are worth knowing.

Pentheus

Your answers are designed to make me curious.

Dionysus

No: 475

our mysteries abhor an unbelieving man.

Pentheus

You say you saw the god. What form did he assume?

Dionysus

Whatever form he wished. The choice was his,
not mine.

Pentheus

You evade the question.

Dionysus

Talk sense to a fool
and he calls you foolish.

Pentheus

Have you introduced your rites   480
in other cities too? Or is Thebes the first?

Dionysus

Foreigners everywhere now dance for Dionysus.

Pentheus

They are more ignorant than Greeks.

Dionysus

In this matter
they are not. Customs differ.

Pentheus

Do you hold your rites
during the day or night?

Dionysus

Mostly by night.   485
The darkness is well suited to devotion.

Pentheus

Better suited to lechery and seducing women.

Dionysus

You can find debauchery by daylight too.

Pentheus

You shall regret these clever answers.

Dionysus

And you,
your stupid blasphemies.

Pentheus

What a bold bacchant!   490
You wrestle well—when it comes to words.

Dionysus

Tell me,
what punishment do you propose?

Pentheus

First of all,
I shall cut off your girlish curls.

Dionysus

My hair is holy.
My curls belong to god.

(Pentheus shears away the god's curls.)

Pentheus

Second, you will surrender
your wand.

Dionysus

You take it. It belongs to Dionysus.

495

(Pentheus takes the thyrsus.)

Pentheus

Last, I shall place you under guard and confine you
in the palace.

Dionysus

The god himself will set me free
whenever I wish.

Pentheus

You will be with your women in prison
when you call on him for help.

Dionysus

He is here now
and sees what I endure from you.

Pentheus

Where is he?
I cannot see him.

500

Dionysus

With me. Your blasphemies
have made you blind.

Pentheus (to attendants)

Seize him. He is mocking me
and Thebes.

Dionysus

         I give you sober warning, fools:
place no chains on *me*.

Pentheus

              But *I* say: chain him.
And I am the stronger here.

Dionysus

                  You do not know   505
the limits of your strength. You do not know
what you do. You do not know who you are.

Pentheus

I am Pentheus, the son of Echion and Agave.

Dionysus

Pentheus: you shall repent that name.

Pentheus

                    Off with him.
Chain his hands; lock him in the stables by the palace.
Since he desires the darkness, give him what he wants.   510
Let him dance down there in the dark.

        *(As the attendants bind Dionysus' hands, the Chorus
            beats on its drums with increasing agitation
               as though to emphasize the sacrilege.)*
                    As for these women,
your accomplices in making trouble here,
I shall have them sold as slaves or put to work
at my looms. That will silence their drums.

                          (Exit Pentheus.)

Dionysus

                    I go,   515
though not to suffer, since that cannot be.
But Dionysus whom you outrage by your acts,

who you deny is god, will call you to account.
When you set chains on me, you manacle the god.

(*Exeunt attendants with Dionysus captive.*)

Chorus

—O Dirce, holy river,   520
  child of Achelöus' water,
  yours the springs that welcomed once
  divinity, the son of Zeus!
  For Zeus the father snatched his son
  from deathless flame, crying: 525
  Dithyrambus, come!
  Enter my male womb.
  I name you Bacchus and to Thebes
  proclaim you by that name.
  But now, O blessèd Dirce,   530
  you banish me when to your banks I come,
  crowned with ivy, bringing revels.
  O Dirce, why am I rejected?
  By the clustered grapes I swear,
  by Dionysus' wine,   535
  someday you shall come to know
     the name of *Bromius!*

—With fury, with fury, he rages,
  Pentheus, son of Echion,   540
  born of the breed of Earth,
  spawned by the dragon, whelped by Earth!
  Inhuman, a rabid beast,
  a giant in wildness raging,
  storming, defying the children of heaven.
  He has threatened me with bonds   545
  though my body is bound to god.
  He cages my comrades with chains;
  he has cast them in prison darkness.
  O lord, son of Zeus, do you see?   550

O Dionysus, do you see
how in shackles we are held
unbreakably, in the bonds of oppressors?
Descend from Olympus, lord!
Come, whirl your wand of gold
and quell with death this beast of blood   555
whose violence abuses man and god
   outrageously.

—O lord, where do you wave your wand
among the running companies of god?
There on Nysa, mother of beasts?
There on the ridges of Corycia?
Or there among the forests of Olympus   560
where Orpheus fingered his lyre
and mustered with music the trees,
mustered the wilderness beasts?
O Pieria, you are blessed!   565
Evius honors you. He comes to dance,
bringing his Bacchae, fording the race
where Axios runs, bringing his Maenads   570
whirling over Lydias,
generous father of rivers
and famed for his lovely waters
that fatten a land of good horses.   575

      (*Thunder and lightning. The earth trembles.*
         The Chorus is crazed with fear.)

Dionysus (*from within*)

  Ho!
  Hear me! Ho, Bacchae!
  Ho, Bacchae! Hear my cry!

Chorus

  Who cries?
  Who calls me with that cry
  of Evius? Where are you, lord?

Dionysus

Ho! Again I cry—
the son of Zeus and Semele!   580

Chorus

O lord, lord Bromius!
Bromius, come to us now!

Dionysus

Let the earthquake come! Shatter the floor of the world!   585

Chorus

—Look there, how the palace of Pentheus totters.
—Look, the palace is collapsing!
—Dionysus is within. Adore him!
—We adore him!   590
—Look there!
            —Above the pillars, how the great stones
      gape and crack!
                  —Listen. Bromius cries his victory!

Dionysus

Launch the blazing thunderbolt of god! O lightnings,
come! Consume with flame the palace of Pentheus!   595

            (*A burst of lightning flares across the façade of the palace*
                        and tongues of flame spurt up from the tomb of
                        Semele. Then a great crash of thunder.)

Chorus

Ah,
look how the fire leaps up
on the holy tomb of Semele,
the flame of Zeus of Thunders,
his lightnings, still alive,
blazing where they fell!
Down, Maenads,   600
fall to the ground in awe! He walks
among the ruins he has made!

He has brought the high house low!
He comes, our god, the son of Zeus!

> (*The Chorus falls to the ground in oriental fashion, bowing
> their heads in the direction of the palace. A hush;
> then Dionysus appears, lightly picking his way
> among the rubble. Calm and smiling still,
> he speaks to the Chorus with a solic-
> itude approaching banter.*)

Dionysus

What, women of Asia? Were you so overcome with fright
you fell to the ground? I think then you must have seen   605
how Bacchus jostled the palace of Pentheus. But come, rise.
Do not be afraid.

Coryphaeus

       O greatest light of our holy revels,
how glad I am to see your face! Without you I was lost.

Dionysus

Did you despair when they led me away to cast me down   610
in the darkness of Pentheus' prison?

Coryphaeus

          What else could I do?
Where would I turn for help if something happened to you?
But how did you escape that godless man?

Dionysus

              With ease.
No effort was required.

Coryphaeus

       But the manacles on your wrists?   615

Dionysus

There I, in turn, humiliated him, outrage for outrage.
He seemed to think that he was chaining me but never once

so much as touched my hands. He fed on his desires.
Inside the stable he intended as my jail, instead of me,
he found a bull and tried to rope its knees and hooves.
He was panting desperately, biting his lips with his teeth, 620
his whole body drenched with sweat, while I sat nearby,
quietly watching. But at that moment Bacchus came,
shook the palace and touched his mother's grave with tongues
of fire. Imagining the palace was in flames,
Pentheus went rushing here and there, shouting to his slaves 625
to bring him water. Every hand was put to work: in vain.
Then, afraid I might escape, he suddenly stopped short,
drew his sword and rushed to the palace. There, it seems,
Bromius had made a shape, a phantom which resembled me, 630
within the court. Bursting in, Pentheus thrust and stabbed
at that thing of gleaming air as though he thought it me.
And then, once again, the god humiliated him.
He razed the palace to the ground where it lies, shattered
in utter ruin—his reward for my imprisonment.
At that bitter sight, Pentheus dropped his sword, exhausted 635
by the struggle. A man, a man, and nothing more,
yet he presumed to wage a war with god.

For my part,

I left the palace quietly and made my way outside.
For Pentheus I care nothing.

But judging from the sound

of tramping feet inside the court, I think our man
will soon be here. What, I wonder, will he have to say? 640
But let him bluster. I shall not be touched to rage.
Wise men know constraint: our passions are controlled.

(*Enter Pentheus, stamping heavily, from the ruined palace.*)

Pentheus

But this is mortifying. That stranger, that man
I clapped in irons, has escaped.

(*He catches sight of Dionysus.*)

What! *You?*
Well, what do you have to say for yourself?
How did you escape? Answer me.

Dionysus

Your anger
walks too heavily. Tread lightly here.

Pentheus

How did you escape?

Dionysus

Don't you remember?
Someone, I said, would set me free.

Pentheus

Someone?
But who? Who is this mysterious someone?

Dionysus

[He who makes the grape grow its clusters
for mankind.]

Pentheus

A splendid contribution, that.

Dionysus

You disparage the gift that is his chiefest glory.

Pentheus

[If I catch him here, he will not escape my anger.]
I shall order every gate in every tower
to be bolted tight.

Dionysus

And so? Could not a god
hurdle your city walls?

Pentheus

You are clever—very—
but not where it counts.

Dionysus

Where it counts the most,
there I *am* clever.

(*Enter a messenger, a herdsman from Mount Cithaeron.*)
But hear this messenger
who brings you news from the mountain of Cithaeron.
We shall remain where we are. Do not fear:
we will not run away.

Messenger

Pentheus, king of Thebes,   660
I come from Cithaeron where the gleaming flakes of snow
fall on and on forever—

Pentheus

Get to the point.
What is your message, man?

Messenger

Sir, I have seen
the holy Maenads, the women who ran barefoot   665
and crazy from the city, and I wanted to report
to you and Thebes what weird fantastic things,
what miracles and more than miracles,
these women do. But may I speak freely
in my own way and words, or make it short?
I fear the harsh impatience of your nature, sire,   670
too kingly and too quick to anger.

Pentheus

Speak freely.
You have my promise: I shall not punish you.
Displeasure with a man who speaks the truth is wrong.
However, the more terrible this tale of yours,
that much more terrible will be the punishment   675
I impose upon that man who taught our womenfolk
this strange new magic.

Messenger

                  About that hour
when the sun lets loose its light to warm the earth,
our grazing herds of cows had just begun to climb
the path along the mountain ridge. Suddenly
I saw three companies of dancing women,   680
one led by Autonoë, the second captained
by your mother Agave, while Ino led the third.
There they lay in the deep sleep of exhaustion,
some resting on boughs of fir, others sleeping
where they fell, here and there among the oak leaves—   685
but all modestly and soberly, not, as you think,
drunk with wine, nor wandering, led astray
by the music of the flute, to hunt their Aphrodite
through the woods.
                  But your mother heard the lowing
of our hornèd herds, and springing to her feet,   690
gave a great cry to waken them from sleep.
And they too, rubbing the bloom of soft sleep
from their eyes, rose up lightly and straight—
a lovely sight to see: all as one,
the old women and the young and the unmarried girls.
First they let their hair fall loose, down   695
over their shoulders, and those whose straps had slipped
fastened their skins of fawn with writhing snakes
that licked their cheeks. Breasts swollen with milk,
new mothers who had left their babies behind at home
nestled gazelles and young wolves in their arms,   700
suckling them. Then they crowned their hair with leaves,
ivy and oak and flowering bryony. One woman
struck her thyrsus against a rock and a fountain
of cool water came bubbling up. Another drove   705
her fennel in the ground, and where it struck the earth,
at the touch of god, a spring of wine poured out.
Those who wanted milk scratched at the soil
with bare fingers and the white milk came welling up. 710

Pure honey spurted, streaming, from their wands.
If you had been there and seen these wonders for yourself,
you would have gone down on your knees and prayed
to the god you now deny.

                   We cowherds and shepherds
gathered in small groups, wondering and arguing   715
among ourselves at these fantastic things,
the awful miracles those women did.
But then a city fellow with the knack of words
rose to his feet and said: "All you who live
upon the pastures of the mountain, what do you say?
Shall we earn a little favor with King Pentheus   720
by hunting his mother Agave out of the revels?"
Falling in with his suggestion, we withdrew
and set ourselves in ambush, hidden by the leaves
among the undergrowth. Then at a signal
all the Bacchae whirled their wands for the revels
to begin. With one voice they cried aloud:
"*O Iacchus! Son of Zeus!*" "*O Bromius!*" they cried   725
until the beasts and all the mountain seemed
wild with divinity. And when they ran,
everything ran with them.

                It happened, however,
that Agave ran near the ambush where I lay
concealed. Leaping up, I tried to seize her,   730
but she gave a cry: "Hounds who run with me,
men are hunting us down! Follow, follow me!
Use your wands for weapons."

                 At this we fled
and barely missed being torn to pieces by the women.
Unarmed, they swooped down upon the herds of cattle   735
grazing there on the green of the meadow. And then
you could have seen a single woman with bare hands
tear a fat calf, still bellowing with fright,
in two, while others clawed the heifers to pieces.
There were ribs and cloven hooves scattered everywhere,   740

and scraps smeared with blood hung from the fir trees.
And bulls, their raging fury gathered in their horns,
lowered their heads to charge, then fell, stumbling
to the earth, pulled down by hordes of women   745
and stripped of flesh and skin more quickly, sire,
than you could blink your royal eyes. Then,
carried up by their own speed, they flew like birds
across the spreading fields along Asopus' stream
where most of all the ground is good for harvesting.   750
Like invaders they swooped on Hysiae
and on Erythrae in the foothills of Cithaeron.
Everything in sight they pillaged and destroyed.
They snatched the children from their homes. And when
they piled their plunder on their backs, it stayed in place,   755
untied. Nothing, neither bronze nor iron,
fell to the dark earth. Flames flickered
in their curls and did not burn them. Then the villagers,
furious at what the women did, took to arms.
And *there*, sire, was something terrible to see.   760
For the men's spears were pointed and sharp, and yet
drew no blood, whereas the wands the women threw
inflicted wounds. And then the men *ran*,
routed by women! Some god, I say, was with them.
The Bacchae then returned where they had started,   765
by the springs the god had made, and washed their hands
while the snakes licked away the drops of blood
that dabbled their cheeks.
                              Whoever this god may be,
sire, welcome him to Thebes. For he is great
in many other ways as well. It was he,   770
or so they say, who gave to mortal men
the gift of lovely wine by which our suffering
is stopped. And if there is no god of wine,
there is no love, no Aphrodite either,
nor other pleasure left to men.

                                        (*Exit messenger.*)

Coryphaeus

I tremble   775
to speak the words of freedom before the tyrant.
But let the truth be told: there is no god
greater than Dionysus.

Pentheus

Like a blazing fire
this Bacchic violence spreads. It comes too close.
We are disgraced, humiliated in the eyes
of Hellas. This is no time for hesitation.   780

(*He turns to an attendant.*)

You there. Go down quickly to the Electran gates
and order out all heavy-armored infantry;
call up the fastest troops among our cavalry,
the mobile squadrons and the archers. We march
against the Bacchae! Affairs are out of hand   785
when we tamely endure such conduct in our women.

(*Exit attendant.*)

Dionysus

Pentheus, you do not hear, or else you disregard
my words of warning. You have done me wrong,
and yet, in spite of that, I warn you once
again: do not take arms against a god.
Stay quiet here. Bromius will not let you   790
drive his women from their revels on the mountain.

Pentheus

Don't you lecture me. You escaped from prison.
Or shall I punish you again?

Dionysus

If I were you,
I would offer him a sacrifice, not rage
and kick against necessity, a man defying   795
god.

Pentheus

      I shall give your god the sacrifice
that he deserves. His victims will be his women.
I shall make a great slaughter in the woods of Cithaeron.

Dionysus

  You will all be routed, shamefully defeated,
when their wands of ivy turn back your shields
of bronze.

Pentheus

        It is hopeless to wrestle with this man.   800
Nothing on earth will make him hold his tongue.

Dionysus

                             Friend,
you can still save the situation.

Pentheus

               How?
By accepting orders from my own slaves?

Dionysus

                   No.
I undertake to lead the women back to Thebes.
Without bloodshed.

Pentheus

          This is some trap.

Dionysus

                  A trap?   805
How so, if I save you by my own devices?

Pentheus

                   I know.
You and they have conspired to establish your rites
forever.

Dionysus

      True, I *have* conspired—with god.

Pentheus

Bring my armor, someone. And *you* stop talking.   810

> (*Pentheus strides toward the left, but when he is almost
> offstage, Dionysus calls imperiously to him.*)

Dionysus
    Wait!
Would you like to *see* their revels on the mountain?

Pentheus

I would pay a great sum to see that sight.

Dionysus

Why are you so passionately curious?

Pentheus

                                        Of course
I'd be sorry to see them drunk—

Dionysus

                                But for all your sorrow,   815
you'd like very much to see them?

Pentheus

                                Yes, very much.
I could crouch beneath the fir trees, out of sight.

Dionysus

But if you try to hide, they may track you down.

Pentheus

Your point is well taken. I will go openly.

Dionysus

Shall I lead you there now? Are you ready to go?

Pentheus

The sooner the better. The loss of even a moment   820
would be disappointing now.

Dionysus

                 First, however,
you must dress yourself in women's clothes.

Pentheus

                           What?
You want *me*, a man, to wear a woman's dress. But why?

Dionysus

If they knew you were a man, they would kill you instantly.

Pentheus

True. You are an old hand at cunning, I see.

Dionysus

Dionysus taught me everything I know.   825

Pentheus

Your advice is to the point. What I fail to see
is what we do.

Dionysus

             I shall go inside with you
and help you dress.

Pentheus

             Dress? In a *woman's* dress,
you mean? I would die of shame.

Dionysus

                  Very well.
Then you no longer hanker to see the Maenads?

Pentheus

What is this costume I must wear?

Dionysus

                On your head   830
I shall set a wig with long curls.

Pentheus

                  And then?

Dionysus

Next, robes to your feet and a net for your hair.

Pentheus

Yes? Go on.

Dionysus

          Then a thyrsus for your hand
and a skin of dappled fawn.

Pentheus

                      I could not bear it.   835
I *cannot* bring myself to dress in women's clothes.

Dionysus

Then you must fight the Bacchae. That means bloodshed

Pentheus

Right. First we must go and reconnoiter.

Dionysus

Surely a wiser course than that of hunting bad
with worse.

Pentheus

          But how can we pass through the city
without being seen?

Dionysus

                We shall take deserted streets.   840
I will lead the way.

Pentheus

              Any way you like,
provided those women of Bacchus don't jeer at me.
First, however, I shall ponder your advice,
whether to go or not.

Dionysus
                    Do as you please.
I am ready, whatever you decide.

Pentheus
                         Yes.
Either I shall march with my army to the mountain   845
or act on your advice.

                              (*Exit Pentheus into the palace.*)

Dionysus
                    Women, our prey now thrashes
in the net we threw. He shall see the Bacchae
and pay the price with death.
                              O Dionysus,
now action rests with you. And you are near.
Punish this man. But first distract his wits;   850
bewilder him with madness. For sane of mind
this man would never wear a woman's dress;
but obsess his soul and he will not refuse.
After those threats with which he was so fierce,
I want him made the laughingstock of Thebes,
paraded through the streets, a woman.
                              Now   855
I shall go and costume Pentheus in the clothes
which he must wear to Hades when he dies, butchered
by the hands of his mother. He shall come to know
Dionysus, son of Zeus, consummate god,   860
most terrible, and yet most gentle, to mankind.

                              (*Exit Dionysus into the palace.*)

Chorus
—When shall I dance once more
    with bare feet the all-night dances,
    tossing my head for joy
    in the damp air, in the dew,   865
    as a running fawn might frisk
    for the green joy of the wide fields,

free from fear of the hunt,
free from the circling beaters 870
and the nets of woven mesh
and the hunters hallooing on
their yelping packs? And then, hard pressed,
she sprints with the quickness of wind,
bounding over the marsh, leaping
to frisk, leaping for joy, 875
gay with the green of the leaves,
to dance for joy in the forest,
to dance where the darkness is deepest,
  where no man is.

—What is wisdom? What gift of the gods
is held in honor like this:
to hold your hand victorious
over the heads of those you hate? 880
Honor is precious forever.

—Slow but unmistakable
the might of the gods moves on.
It punishes that man,
infatuate of soul
and hardened in his pride, 885
who disregards the gods.
The gods are crafty:
they lie in ambush
a long step of time
to hunt the unholy. 890
Beyond the old beliefs,
no thought, no act shall go.
Small, small is the cost
to believe in this:
whatever is god is strong;
whatever long time has sanctioned,
that is a law forever;
the law tradition makes 895
is the law of nature.

—What is wisdom? What gift of the gods
   is held in honor like this:
   to hold your hand victorious
   over the heads of those you hate?   900
   Honor is precious forever.

—Blessèd is he who escapes a storm at sea,
   who comes home to his harbor.
—Blessèd is he who emerges from under affliction.
—In various ways one man outraces another in the
   race for wealth and power.   905
—Ten thousand men possess ten thousand hopes.
—A few bear fruit in happiness; the others go awry.
—But he who garners day by day the good of life,   910
   he is happiest. Blessèd is he.

> (*Re-enter Dionysus from the palace. At the threshold*
> *he turns and calls back to Pentheus.*)

Dionysus

Pentheus if you are still so curious to see
forbidden sights, so bent on evil still,
come out. Let us see you in your woman's dress,
disguised in Maenad clothes so you may go and spy   915
upon your mother and her company.

> (*Enter Pentheus from the palace. He wears a long linen dress*
> *which partially conceals his fawn-skin. He carries a thyrsus*
> *in his hand; on his head he wears a wig with long blond*
> *curls bound by a snood. He is dazed and completely in*
> *the power of the god who has now possessed him.*)

                    Why,
you look exactly like one of the daughters of Cadmus.

Pentheus

I seem to see two suns blazing in the heavens.
And now two Thebes, two cities, and each
with seven gates. And you—you are a bull   920

who walks before me there. Horns have sprouted
from your head. Have you always been a beast?
But now I see a bull.

Dionysus

It is the god you see.
Though hostile formerly, he now declares a truce
and goes with us. You see what you could not
when you were blind.

Pentheus (coyly primping)

Do I look like anyone?   925
Like Ino or my mother Agave?

Dionysus

So much alike
I almost might be seeing one of them. But look:
one of your curls has come loose from under the snood
where I tucked it.

Pentheus

It must have worked loose
when I was dancing for joy and shaking my head.   930

Dionysus

Then let me be your maid and tuck it back.
Hold still.

Pentheus

Arrange it. I am in your hands
completely.

(Dionysus tucks the curl back under the snood.)

Dionysus

And now your strap has slipped. Yes,   935
and your robe hangs askew at the ankles.

Pentheus (bending backward to look)

I think so.
At least on my right leg. But on the left the hem
lies straight.

« 196 »

Dionysus

        You will think me the best of friends
when you see to your surprise how chaste the Bacchae are.   940

Pentheus

But to be a real Bacchante, should I hold
the wand in my right hand? Or this way?

Dionysus

                        No.
In your right hand. And raise it as you raise
your right foot. I commend your change of heart.

Pentheus

Could I lift Cithaeron up, do you think?   945
Shoulder the cliffs, Bacchae and all?

Dionysus

                   If you wanted.
Your mind was once unsound, but now you think
as sane men do.

Pentheus

            Should we take crowbars with us?
Or should I put my shoulder to the cliffs   950
and heave them up?

Dionysus

             What? And destroy the haunts
of the nymphs, the holy groves where Pan plays
his woodland pipe?

Pentheus

             You are right. In any case,
women should not be mastered by brute strength.
I will hide myself beneath the firs instead.

Dionysus

You will find all the ambush you deserve,   955
creeping up to spy on the Maenads.

Pentheus

Think.

I can see them already, there among the bushes,
mating like birds, caught in the toils of love.

Dionysus

Exactly. This is your mission: you go to watch.
You may surprise them—or they may surprise you.   960

Pentheus

Then lead me through the very heart of Thebes,
since I, alone of all this city, dare to go.

Dionysus

You and you alone will suffer for your city.
A great ordeal awaits you. But you are worthy
of your fate. I shall lead you safely there;   965
someone else shall bring you back.

Pentheus

Yes, my mother.

Dionysus

An example to all men.

Pentheus

It is for that I go.

Dionysus

You will be carried home—

Pentheus

O luxury!

Dionysus

cradled in your mother's arms.

Pentheus

You will spoil me.

Dionysus

I *mean* to spoil you.

Pentheus

I go to my reward. 970

Dionysus

You are an extraordinary young man, and you go
to an extraordinary experience. You shall win
a glory towering to heaven and usurping
god's.

(*Exit Pentheus.*)

Agave and you daughters of Cadmus,
reach out your hands! I bring this young man
to a great ordeal. The victor? Bromius. 975
Bromius—and I. The rest the event shall show.

(*Exit Dionysus.*)

Chorus

—Run to the mountain, fleet hounds of madness!
Run, run to the revels of Cadmus' daughters!
Sting them against the man in women's clothes, 980
the madman who spies on the Maenads, who peers
from behind the rocks, who spies from a vantage!
His mother shall see him first. She will cry 985
to the Maenads: "Who is this spy who has come
to the mountains to peer at the mountain-revels
of the women of Thebes? What bore him, Bacchae?
This man was born of no woman. Some lioness
gave him birth, some one of the Libyan gorgons!" 990

—O Justice, principle of order, spirit of custom,
come! Be manifest; reveal yourself with a sword!
Stab through the throat that godless man,
the mocker who goes, flouting custom and outraging god!
O Justice, stab the evil earth-born spawn of Echion! 995

—Uncontrollable, the unbeliever goes,
in spitting rage, rebellious and amok,
madly assaulting the mysteries of god,
profaning the rites of the mother of god.

Against the unassailable he runs, with rage   1000
obsessed. Headlong he runs to death.
For death the gods exact, curbing by that bit
the mouths of men. They humble us with death
that we remember what we are who are not god,
but men. We run to death. Wherefore, I say,
accept, accept:
humility is wise; humility is blest.
But what the world calls wise I do not want.   1005
Elsewhere the chase. I hunt another game,
those great, those manifest, those certain goals,
achieving which, our mortal lives are blest.
Let these things be the quarry of my chase:
purity; humility; an unrebellious soul,
accepting all. Let me go the customary way,
the timeless, honored, beaten path of those who walk
with reverence and awe beneath the sons of heaven.   1010

—O Justice, principle of order, spirit of custom,
come! Be manifest; reveal yourself with a sword!
Stab through the throat that godless man,
the mocker who goes, flouting custom and outraging god!
O Justice, destroy the evil earth-born sprawn of Echion!   1015

—O Dionysus, reveal yourself a bull! Be manifest,
a snake with darting heads, a lion breathing fire!
O Bacchus, come! Come with your smile!
Cast your noose about this man who hunts
your Bacchae! Bring him down, trampled   1020
underfoot by the murderous herd of your Maenads!

(*Enter a messenger from Cithaeron.*)

Messenger

How prosperous in Hellas these halls once were,
this house founded by Cadmus, the stranger from Sidon   1025
who sowed the dragon seed in the land of the snake!

I am a slave and nothing more, yet even so
I mourn the fortunes of this fallen house.

Coryphaeus

                                  What is it?
Is there news of the Bacchae?

Messenger

                        This is my news:
Pentheus, the son of Echion, is dead.   1030

Coryphaeus

All hail to Bromius! Our god is a great god!

Messenger

What is this you say, women? You dare to rejoice
at these disasters which destroy this house?

Coryphaeus

I am no Greek. I hail my god
in my own way. No longer need I
shrink with fear of prison.   1035

Messenger

If you suppose this city is so short of men—

Coryphaeus

Dionysus, Dionysus, not Thebes,
has power over me.

Messenger

Your feelings might be forgiven, then. But this,
this exultation in disaster—it is not right.   1040

Coryphaeus

Tell us how the mocker died.
How was he killed?

Messenger

There were three of us in all: Pentheus and I,
attending my master, and that stranger who volunteered
his services as guide. Leaving behind us
the last outlying farms of Thebes, we forded
the Asopus and struck into the barren scrubland   1045
of Cithaeron.

           There in a grassy glen we halted,
unmoving, silent, without a word,
so we might see but not be seen. From that vantage,   1050
in a hollow cut from the sheer rock of the cliffs,
a place where water ran and the pines grew dense
with shade, we saw the Maenads sitting, their hands
busily moving at their happy tasks. Some
wound the stalks of their tattered wands with tendrils   1055
of fresh ivy; others, frisking like fillies
newly freed from the painted bridles, chanted
in Bacchic songs, responsively.

           But Pentheus—
unhappy man—could not quite see the companies
of women. "Stranger," he said, "from where I stand,
I cannot see these counterfeited Maenads.   1060
But if I climbed that towering fir that overhangs
the banks, then I could see their shameless orgies
better."

           And now the stranger worked a miracle.
Reaching for the highest branch of a great fir,
he bent it down, down, down to the dark earth,   1065
till it was curved the way a taut bow bends
or like a rim of wood when forced about the circle
of a wheel. Like that he forced that mountain fir
down to the ground. No mortal could have done it.
Then he seated Pentheus at the highest tip   1070
and with his hands let the trunk rise straightly up,
slowly and gently, lest it throw its rider.
And the tree rose, towering to heaven, with my master

huddled at the top. And now the Maenads saw him
more clearly than he saw them. But barely had they seen,   1075
when the stranger vanished and there came a great voice
out of heaven—Dionysus', it must have been—
crying: "Women, I bring you the man who has mocked
at you and me and at our holy mysteries.   1080
Take vengeance upon him." And as he spoke
a flash of awful fire bound earth and heaven.
The high air hushed, and along the forest glen
the leaves hung still; you could hear no cry of beasts.   1085
The Bacchae heard that voice but missed its words,
and leaping up, they stared, peering everywhere.
Again that voice. And now they knew his cry,
the clear command of god. And breaking loose
like startled doves, through grove and torrent,   1090
over jagged rocks, they flew, their feet maddened
by the breath of god. And when they saw my master
perching in his tree, they climbed a great stone   1095
that towered opposite his perch and showered him
with stones and javelins of fir, while the others
hurled their wands. And yet they missed their target,
poor Pentheus in his perch, barely out of reach   1100
of their eager hands, treed, unable to escape.
Finally they splintered branches from the oaks
and with those bars of wood tried to lever up the tree
by prying at the roots. But every effort failed.   1105
Then Agave cried out: "Maenads, make a circle
about the trunk and grip it with your hands.
Unless we take this climbing beast, he will reveal
the secrets of the god." With that, thousands of hands
tore the fir tree from the earth, and down, down   1110
from his high perch fell Pentheus, tumbling
to the ground, sobbing and screaming as he fell,
for he knew his end was near. His own mother,
like a priestess with her victim, fell upon him
first. But snatching off his wig and snood   1115

so she would recognize his face, he touched her cheeks,
screaming, *"No, no, Mother! I am Pentheus,*
your own son, the child you bore to Echion!
Pity me, spare me, Mother! I have done a wrong,   1120
but do not kill your own son for my offense."
But she was foaming at the mouth, and her crazed eyes
rolling with frenzy. She was mad, stark mad,
possessed by Bacchus. Ignoring his cries of pity,
she seized his left arm at the wrist; then, planting   1125
her foot upon his chest, she pulled, wrenching away
the arm at the shoulder—not by her own strength,
for the god had put inhuman power in her hands.
Ino, meanwhile, on the other side, was scratching off
his flesh. Then Autonoë and the whole horde   1130
of Bacchae swarmed upon him. Shouts everywhere,
he screaming with what little breath was left,
they shrieking in triumph. One tore off an arm,
another a foot still warm in its shoe. His ribs
were clawed clean of flesh and every hand   1135
was smeared with blood as they played ball with scraps
of Pentheus' body.

                The pitiful remains lie scattered,
one piece among the sharp rocks, others
lying lost among the leaves in the depths
of the forest. His mother, picking up his head,   1140
impaled it on her wand. She seems to think it is
some mountain lion's head which she carries in triumph
through the thick of Cithaeron. Leaving her sisters
at the Maenad dances, she is coming here, gloating
over her grisly prize. She calls upon Bacchus: 1145
he is her "fellow-huntsman," "comrade of the chase,
crowned with victory." But all the victory
she carries home is her own grief.

                        Now,
before Agave returns, let me leave
this scene of sorrow. Humility,

a sense of reverence before the sons of heaven—   1150
of all the prizes that a mortal man might win,
these, I say, are wisest; these are best.

                              (*Exit Messenger.*)

Chorus

—We dance to the glory of Bacchus!
   We dance to the death of Pentheus,
   the death of the spawn of the dragon!   1155
      He dressed in woman's dress;
      he took the lovely thyrsus;
      it waved him down to death,
         led by a bull to Hades.
   Hail, Bacchae! Hail, women of Thebes!   1160
   Your victory is fair, fair the prize,
         this famous prize of grief!
   Glorious the game! To fold your child
   in your arms, streaming with his blood!

Coryphaeus

   But look: there comes Pentheus' mother, Agave,   1165
   running wild-eyed toward the palace.
                              —Welcome,
   welcome to the reveling band of the god of joy!

      (*Enter Agave with other Bacchantes. She is covered with blood
         and carries the head of Pentheus impaled upon her thyrsus.*)

Agave

   Bacchae of Asia—

Chorus

                  Speak, speak.

Agave

   We bring this branch to the palace,
   this fresh-cut spray from the mountains.   1170
   Happy was the hunting.

Chorus

                    I see.
I welcome our fellow-reveler of god.

Agave

The whelp of a wild mountain lion,
and snared by me without a noose.
Look, look at the prize I bring.   1175

Chorus

Where was he caught?

Agave

                    On Cithaeron—

Chorus

On Cithaeron?

Agave

                    Our prize was killed.

Chorus

Who killed him?

Agave

                    I struck him first.
The Maenads call me "Agave the blest."   1180

Chorus

And then?

Agave

          Cadmus'—

Chorus

                    Cadmus'?

Agave

                              Daughters.
After me, they reached the prey.
After me. Happy was the hunting.

Chorus

Happy indeed.

Agave

   Then share my glory,
share the feast.

Chorus

   Share, unhappy woman?

Agave

See, the whelp is young and tender.   1185
Beneath the soft mane of its hair,
the down is blooming on the cheeks.

Chorus

With that mane he *looks* a beast.

Agave

Our god is wise. Cunningly, cleverly,   1190
Bacchus the hunter lashed the Maenads
against his prey.

Chorus

   Our king is a hunter.

Agave

You praise me now?

Chorus

    I praise you.

Agave

The men of Thebes—

Chorus

   And Pentheus, your son?

Agave

Will praise his mother. She caught   1195
a great quarry, this lion's cub.

Chorus

    Extraordinary catch.

Agave

                   Extraordinary skill. .

Chorus

    You are proud?

Agave

                Proud and happy.
I have won the trophy of the chase,
a great prize, manifest to all.

Coryphaeus

    Then, poor woman, show the citizens of Thebes   1200
this great prize, this trophy you have won
in the hunt.

                (*Agave proudly exhibits her thyrsus with the head
                    of Pentheus impaled upon the point.*)

Agave

           You citizens of this towered city,
men of Thebes, behold the trophy of your women's
hunting! *This* is the quarry of our chase, taken
not with nets nor spears of bronze but by the white   1205
and delicate hands of women. What are they worth,
your boastings now and all that uselessness
your armor is, since we, with our bare hands,
captured this quarry and tore its bleeding body
limb from limb?

              —But where is my father Cadmus?   1210
He should come. And my son. Where is Pentheus?
Fetch him. I will have him set his ladder up
against the wall and, there upon the beam,
nail the head of this wild lion I have killed
as a trophy of my hunt.

        (*Enter Cadmus, followed by attendants who bear upon
             a bier the dismembered body of Pentheus.*)

Cadmus
                    Follow me, attendants.   1215
Bear your dreadful burden in and set it down,
there before the palace.

                        (*The attendants set down the bier.*)

                    This was Pentheus
whose body, after long and weary searchings
I painfully assembled from Cithaeron's glens
where it lay, scattered in shreads, dismembered
throughout the forest, no two pieces   1220
in a single place.
                    Old Teiresias and I
had returned to Thebes from the orgies on the mountain
before I learned of this atrocious crime
my daughters did. And so I hurried back
to the mountain to recover the body of this boy   1225
murdered by the Maenads. There among the oaks
I found Aristaeus' wife, the mother of Actaeon,
Autonoë, and with her Ino, both
still stung with madness. But Agave, they said,
was on her way to Thebes, still possessed.   1230
And what they said was true, for there she is,
and not a happy sight.

Agave
                    Now, Father,
yours can be the proudest boast of living men.
For you are now the father of the bravest daughters
in the world. All of your daughters are brave,   1235
but I above the rest. I have left my shuttle
at the loom; I raised my sight to higher things—
to hunting animals with my bare hands.
                              You see?
Here in my hands I hold the quarry of my chase,
a trophy for our house. Take it, Father, take it.   1240
Glory in my kill and invite your friends to share

the feast of triumph. For you are blest, Father,
by this great deed I have done.

Cadmus

               This is a grief
so great it knows no size. I cannot look.
This is the awful murder your hands have done.   1245
This, this is the noble victim you have slaughtered
to the gods. And to share a feast like this
you now invite all Thebes and me?

                      O gods,
how terribly I pity you and then myself.
Justly—too, too justly—has lord Bromius,
this god of our own blood, destroyed us all,   1250
every one.

Agave

           How scowling and crabbed is old age
in men. I hope my son takes after his mother
and wins, as she has done, the laurels of the chase
when he goes hunting with the younger men of Thebes.
But all my son can do is quarrel with god.   1255
He should be scolded, Father, and you are the one
who should scold him. Yes, someone call him out
so he can see his mother's triumph.

Cadmus

                  Enough. No more.
When you realize the horror you have done,
you shall suffer terribly. But if with luck   1260
your present madness lasts until you die,
you will seem to have, not having, happiness.

Agave

Why do you reproach me? Is there something wrong?

Cadmus

First raise your eyes to the heavens.

Agave
                         There.   1265
   But why?

Cadmus
          Does it look the same as it did before?
   Or has it changed?

Agave
                    It seems—somehow—clearer,
   brighter than it was before.

Cadmus
                    Do you still feel
   the same flurry inside you?

Agave
                    The same—flurry?
   No, I feel—somehow—calmer. I feel as though—   1270
   my mind were somehow—changing.

Cadmus
                         Can you still hear me?
   Can you answer clearly?

Agave
               No. I have forgotten
   what we were saying, Father.

Cadmus
                    Who was your husband?

Agave
   Echion—a man, they said, born of the dragon seed.

Cadmus
   What was the name of the child you bore your husband?   1275

Agave
   Pentheus.

Cadmus

And whose head do you hold in your hands?

Agave (averting her eyes)

A lion's head—or so the hunters told me.

Cadmus

Look directly at it. Just a quick glance.

Agave

What is it? What am I holding in my hands?   1280

Cadmus

Look more closely still. Study it carefully.

Agave

No! O gods, I see the greatest grief there is.

Cadmus

Does it look like a lion now?

Agave

No, no. It is—
Pentheus' head—I hold—

Cadmus

And mourned by me   1285
before you ever knew.

Agave

But *who* killed him?
Why am *I* holding him?

Cadmus

O savage truth,
what a time to come!

Agave

For god's sake, speak.
My heart is beating with terror.

Cadmus

You killed him.
You and your sisters.

Agave

But where was he killed? 1290
Here at home? Where?

Cadmus

He was killed on Cithaeron,
there where the hounds tore Actaeon to pieces.

Agave

But why? Why had Pentheus gone to Cithaeron?

Cadmus

He went to your revels to mock the god.

Agave

But we—
what were we doing on the mountain?

Cadmus

You were mad. 1295
The whole city was possessed.

Agave

Now, now I see:
Dionysus has destroyed us all.

Cadmus

You outraged him.
You denied that he was truly god.

Agave

Father,
where is my poor boy's body now?

Cadmus

There it is.
I gathered the pieces with great difficulty.

Agave

    Is his body entire? Has he been laid out well?   1300

Cadmus

    [All but the head. The rest is mutilated
    horribly.]

Agave

            But why should Pentheus suffer for my crime?

Cadmus

    He, like you, blasphemed the god. And so
    the god has brought us all to ruin at one blow,
    you, your sisters, and this boy. All our house
    the god as utterly destroyed and, with it,
    me. For I have no sons left, no male heir;   1305
    and I have lived only to see this boy,
    this branch of your own body, most horribly
    and foully killed.

                        (He turns and addresses the corpse.)

               —To you my house looked up.
    Child, you were the stay of my house; you were
    my daughter's son. Of you this city stood in awe.   1310
    No one who once had seen your face dared outrage
    the old man, or if he did, you punished him.
    Now I must go, a banished and dishonored man—
    I, Cadmus the great, who sowed the soldiery
    of Thebes and harvested a great harvest. My son,   1315
    dearest to me of all men—for even dead,
    I count you still the man I love the most—
    never again will your hand touch my chin;
    no more, child, will you hug me and call me
    "Grandfather" and say, "Who is wronging you?   1320
    Does anyone trouble you or vex your heart, old man?
    Tell me, Grandfather, and I will punish him."
    No, now there is grief for me; the mourning

for you; pity for your mother; and for her sisters,
sorrow.
      If there is still any mortal man 1325
who despises or defies the gods, let him look
on this boy's death and believe in the gods.

Coryphaeus

Cadmus, I pity you. Your daughter's son
has died as he deserved, and yet his death
bears hard on you.

[*At this point there is a break in the manuscript of nearly fifty lines.
The following speeches of Agave and Coryphaeus and the first part of
Dionysus' speech have been conjecturally reconstructed from fragments and
later material which made use of the Bacchae. Lines which can plausibly
be assigned to the lacuna are otherwise not indicated. My own inventions
are designed, not to complete the speeches, but to effect a transition between the fragments, and are bracketed. For fuller comment, see the Appendix.—*TRANS.]

Agave

        O Father, now you can see
how everything has changed. I am in anguish now,
tormented, who walked in triumph minutes past,
exulting in my kill. And that prize I carried home
with such pride was my own curse. Upon these hands
I bear the curse of my son's blood. How then
with these accursed hands may I touch his body?
How can I, accursed with such a curse, hold him
to my breast? O gods, what dirge can I sing
[that there might be] a dirge [for every]
broken limb?

. . . .

      Where is a shroud to cover up his corpse?
O my child, what hands will give you proper care
unless with my own hands I lift my curse?

*(She lifts up one of Pentheus' limbs and asks the help of Cadmus
in piecing the body together. She mourns each piece separate-
ly before replacing it on the bier. See Appendix.)*

Come, Father. We must restore his head
to this unhappy boy. As best we can, we shall make
him whole again.
           —O dearest, dearest face!
Pretty boyish mouth! Now with this veil
I shroud your head, gathering with loving care
these mangled bloody limbs, this flesh I brought
to birth

. . . .

Coryphaeus

Let this scene teach those [who see these things:
Dionysus is the son] of Zeus.

(Above the palace Dionysus appears in epiphany.)

Dionysus

               [I am Dionysus,
the son of Zeus, returned to Thebes, revealed,
a god to men.] But the men [of Thebes] blasphemed me.
They slandered me; they said I came of mortal man,
and not content with speaking blasphemies,
[they dared to threaten my person with violence.]
These crimes this people whom I cherished well
did from malice to their benefactor. Therefore,
I now disclose the sufferings in store for them.
Like [enemies], they shall be driven from this city
to other lands; there, submitting to the yoke
of slavery, they shall wear out wretched lives,
captives of war, enduring much indignity.

(He turns to the corpse of Pentheus.)

This man has found the death which he deserved,
torn to pieces among the jagged rocks.
You are my witnesses: he came with outrage;

he attempted to chain my hands, abusing me
[and doing what he should least of all have done.]
And therefore he has rightly perished by the hands
of those who should the least of all have murdered him.
What he suffers, he suffers justly.

       Upon you,
Agave, and on your sisters I pronounce this doom:
you shall leave this city in expiation
of the murder you have done. You are unclean,
and it would be a sacrilege that murderers
should remain at peace beside the graves [of those
whom they have killed].

         (*He turns to Cadmus.*)

. . . .

      Next I shall disclose the trials
which await this man. You, Cadmus, shall be changed   1330
to a serpent, and your wife, the child of Ares,
immortal Harmonia, shall undergo your doom,
a serpent too. With her, it is your fate
to go a journey in a car drawn on by oxen,
leading behind you a great barbarian host.
For thus decrees the oracle of Zeus.
With a host so huge its numbers cannot be counted,   1335
you shall ravage many cities; but when your army
plunders the shrine of Apollo, its homecoming
shall be perilous and hard. Yet in the end
the god Ares shall save Harmonia and you
and bring you both to live among the blest.

  So say I, born of no mortal father,   1340
Dionysus, true son of Zeus. If then,
when you would not, you had muzzled your madness,
you should have an ally now in the son of Zeus.

Cadmus

 We implore you, Dionysus. We have done wrong.

Dionysus

Too late. When there was time, you did not know me.   1345

Cadmus

We have learned. But your sentence is too harsh.

Dionysus

I am a god. I was blasphemed by you.

Cadmus

Gods should be exempt from human passions.

Dionysus

Long ago my father Zeus ordained these things.

Agave

It is fated, Father. We must go.

Dionysus

                          Why then delay?   1350
For you must go.

Cadmus

                  Child, to what a dreadful end
have we all come, you and your wretched sisters
and my unhappy self. An old man, I must go
to live a stranger among barbarian peoples, doomed   1355
to lead against Hellas a motley foreign army.
Transformed to serpents, I and my wife,
Harmonia, the child of Ares, we must captain
spearsmen against the tombs and shrines of Hellas.
Never shall my sufferings end; not even   1360
over Acheron shall I have peace.

Agave (embracing Cadmus)

                    O Father,
to be banished, to live without you!

Cadmus
                              Poor child,
like a white swan warding its weak old father,   1365
why do you clasp those white arms about my neck?

Agave

But banished! Where shall I go?

Cadmus
                              I do not know,
my child. Your father can no longer help you.

Agave

Farewell, my home! City, farewell.
O bridal bed, banished I go,   1370
in misery, I leave you now.

Cadmus

Go, poor child, seek shelter in Aristaeus' house.

Agave

I pity you, Father.

Cadmus
                              And I pity you, my child,
and I grieve for your poor sisters. I pity them.

Agave

Terribly has Dionysus brought   1375
disaster down upon this house.

Dionysus

I was terribly blasphemed,
my name dishonored in Thebes.

Agave

Farewell, Father.

Cadmus

Farewell to you, unhappy child.
Fare well. But you shall find your faring hard. 1380

(*Exit Cadmus.*)

Agave

Lead me, guides, where my sisters wait,
poor sisters of my exile. Let me go
where I shall never see Cithaeron more, 1385
where that accursed hill may not see me,
where I shall find no trace of thyrsus!
That I leave to other Bacchae.

(*Exit Agave with attendants.*)

Chorus

The gods have many shapes.
The gods bring many things
to their accomplishment.
And what was most expected 1390
has not been accomplished.
But god has found his way
for what no man expected.
So ends the play.

APPENDIX TO *THE BACCHAE*

APPENDIX

Reconstruction of the long lacuna (l. 1329) can never be more than conjectural; but it can at least be that. I have attempted it in the conviction that its presence seriously hinders any possible production of the play.

The contents of the lacuna are, at least in outline, tolerably clear. A third-century rhetorician, Apsines, describes the speech of Agave, how she arouses pity by "picking up in her hands each one of her son's limbs and mourning it individually" (see Apsines *Rhet. Gr.* [ed. Walz], ix. 587). Then, according to the hypothesis of the play, Dionysus appears and addresses all, and foretells the future of each one in turn. The manuscript picks up the speech of Dionysus at line 1330 with an account, virtually complete, of the fate of Cadmus. Against this framework, scholars have been able to place a large number of Euripidean lines from the *Christus Patiens*, a twelfth-century cento, made up of lines from at least seven Euripidean plays. The bulk of the lines which fill the lacuna in my translation come from the *C.P.* Some of them are almost certain; others less so; but together they go a long way toward rounding out the gap. Thorough discussion of the lacuna problem may be found in the commentary on line 1329 in Dodds's edition of *The Bacchae*.

The order of my lines is as follows: beginning, *Bacchae*, l. 1329; *C.P.* ll. 1011, 1311, 1312, 1313, 1256, 1122, 1123; Schol. in Ar. Plut. l. 907; *C.P.* ll. 1466, 1467, 1468, 1469, 1470; Pap. Ant. 24 (*Antinoopolis Pap.* I, ed. C. H. Roberts, 1951) and *C.P.* l. 1472. The speech of Coryphaeus: pap. frag. (cf. Dodds, App. I). The speech of Dionysus: *C.P.* ll. 1360–62, 1665–66, 1668–69, 1678–80, 300; Lucian, *Pisc.* 2; *C.P.* ll. 1692, 1664, 1663, 1667, 1674–78, 1690.

CHRONOLOGICAL NOTE ON
THE PLAYS OF EURIPIDES

By Richmond Lattimore

CHRONOLOGICAL NOTE ON THE PLAYS OF EURIPIDES

THE chief data on the life of Euripides have been stated in the General Introduction to Euripides, Volume I in this series, but may be repeated here. They are:

485–480	Birth
455	First competition (including *The Daughters of Pelias*)
441	First victory (titles unknown)
408–407	Migration to Macedon
407–406	Death

Between 455 and 438, the date of *Alcestis*, we have only two performances for Euripides attested, and no extant play, except *Rhesus*, is likely to fall in that period. If these dates are really right, the blankness of the early years is rather surprising and can perhaps best be accounted for by assuming extensive military service.

I go on to give, as best I can, an outline of the extant plays in chronological order. Dates are derived as follows: (*a*) Recorded dates. These are found in ancient manuscripts, whether of Euripides or others. There is every probability that they are reliable, and they have not here been questioned. (*b*) Indications from style. These are chiefly metrical. It is well known that Euripides, as time went on, made freer use of resolution in iambic lines (see my Introduction to *Rhesus* in *Euripides IV*); was more likely to use trochees; and was more likely to use *antilabe*, the interruption of a line by a change of speakers. Such evidence will not date a play precisely, but it is reliable within limits; for instance, on metrical grounds alone, we could have stated that *Medea* (431) could not *possibly* have been written after 420. The implications of other stylistic variations have yet to be fully worked out. (*c*) Indications from content. Allusions to issues of the time are sometimes indicative, sometimes (if precise, as in *Electra*) even conclusive.

Question marks have been prefixed to those titles over which there could regularly be disagreement.

I have wished to keep discussion brief and have avoided the minutiae of scholarship which would be appropriate to a treatise dealing with Greek text.

?455–441   *Rhesus*

It has been doubted whether Euripides wrote this play at all, but if (as I think) he did, it fits best into the period before he achieved the general style familiar from his other preserved plays.

438   *Alcestis*

Date recorded in *Didascalia* (production notes on the manuscript).

431   *Medea*

Date recorded in *Didascalia*.

?429   *The Heracleidae*

The general period would be indicated by the metrical character; the conjectured year from the probable connection with the execution of the ambassadors during the course of the previous year, as explained in the Introduction to this play.

428   *Hippolytus*

Date recorded in *Didascalia*.

?426   *Andromache*

The *Didascalia* give no date. The *Scholia* (ancient notes on the manuscript) indicate that it was not performed at Athens, not at least under the name of Euripides; it may have been given under the name of Democrates. This curious fact prevents me from putting it in the same trilogy with *Hecuba* and *The Cyclops* (see below), as I should otherwise have been tempted to do. Mr. Nims suggests that the treatment of Andromache by the Spartans is based on the actions of the Spartans toward the Plataeans in 427, and I agree. The plausibility of this is perhaps helped a little (for me) by the similarity in situation with Sophocles' *The Women of Trachis*, which on other grounds I should like to place in 425. But all this is admittedly tenuous.

?425 *Hecuba*

There seems to be a reference to the Delian Festival, re-established in the winter of 426–425 (ll. 455 ff.); and Aristophanes parodies line 172 in his *Clouds* (423 B.C.). So too Mr. Arrowsmith dates it 425 or 424; see his Introduction to this play. There has been pretty general agreement about this, and, give or take a year, there is not really much doubt about the date of this play.

?425 *The Cyclops*

Mr. Arrowsmith would make this the satyr play for the set which contained *Hecuba*. I find this attractive, but there is nothing resembling certainty about the matter. Metrical tests are useless when it comes to satyr plays.

?423 *The Suppliant Women*

This is very much a matter of conjecture. The date I suggest is based on the idea that Euripides was thinking of the refusal by the Thebans to permit the Athenians, whom they had defeated at the Battle of Delium, to bury their dead (Thucydides iv. 97–101). This was in the summer of 424 B.C. Mr. Jones dates it 420–415, and he may well be right. The style supports the later date, but not decisively; the metrical habits of Euripides were changing between 425 and 415, but we cannot just fix the stages. I find the bitterly anti-Theban tone unlikely for the period of attempted reconciliation which came in after 423.

?420 *Heracles*

This could come at any time from 422 to 416. Mr. Arrowsmith would put it in 419 or 418. The play uses trochees, which are missing in the earlier complete plays. The lack of anti-Theban polemics is so striking as to make the tone seem (to me) positively conciliatory.

415 *The Trojan Women*

Date recorded by Aelian, *Varia historica* ii. 8.

?414 *Iphigenia in Tauris*

There is no external evidence, but style and structure support this date (see my Introduction to the play in *Euripides II*).

413 *Electra*

Lines 1347–48 are thought by almost everyone to refer to the relief expedition sent by the Athenians to Sicily in the early spring of 413 (Thucydides vii. 20. 2). The metrical character, particularly the absence of trochees, would otherwise have suggested a rather earlier date (see my Introduction to *Rhesus*). Mrs. Vermeule accepts the "traditional" date, and I follow, with only faint misgivings.

412 *Helen*

The date is secure from a combination of statements in the *Scholia* to Aristophanes' *Frogs* and *Thesmophoriazusae*.

?412 *Ion*

Mr. Willetts is content with the limits 420–410, and other good scholars have placed it before *The Trojan Women* and *Electra*, but I cannot believe that it is earlier than these plays. It has the late signs: a high rate of resolution (higher than *Electra*, though not so high as *Helen* or *The Phoenician Women*), abundant trochees and *antilabe*. The reference to Athens as a city where people are frightened (especially people who cannot demonstrate their right to citizenship?—see line 601) would *best* suit 410, after the reactionary revolution in Athens, but would do for any time just after the defeat in Sicily. The metrical style is better for 412.

One might add this consideration: For *Helen* and the lost, but parodied, *Andromeda* which was given along with it (*Scholia* on *Thesmophoriazusae*, l. 1021) Euripides obviously had the services of an actor who could do coloratura parts, and he obviously also had such an actor for *Ion*. We cannot say that 412 is a perfectly firm date for *Ion*, but I would feel pretty confident about narrowing the limits down to 413–410.

?410 *The Phoenician Women*

Presented after *Andromeda* (412), *Scholia* on Aristophanes, *Frogs*, l. 53. The lost *Antiope* and *Hypsipyle* are mentioned in the same connection, which may or may not mean they were given along with it. The particular date 410 has only the slight merit of spacing. It is plain that the "old swan" was immensely productive in the last decade of his life, but it might be better to leave whatever gap we can between the attested productions of 412 and 408.

408   Orestes
The date is from the *Scholia* to line 371.

406–405   *The Bacchae*
Posthumously presented along with *Iphigenia in Aulis* and *Alcmaeon in Corinth* (the latter lost); attested, *Scholia* to Aristophanes, *Frogs*, l. 67. The plays of course may well have been, and probably were, written in 407.

406–405   *Iphigenia in Aulis*
See under *The Bacchae*.

It will thus be seen that, except for the early period before 438 B.C., we have a reasonably good idea of the chronology for the plays of Euripides, which we owe to a combination of data. One could only wish that the objective evidence for Sophocles were half as good. I hope that students will also agree that, when it comes to Euripides' views about war, politics, women, domestics, and the gods, it is wiser to interpret him always within the limits of the particular piece which is being considered; for his opinions were not always the same from play to play.

THE COMPLETE GREEK TRAGEDIES

AESCHYLUS · I *ORESTEIA*

Translated and with an Introduction by Richmond Lattimore

Agamemnon
The Libation Bearers
The Eumenides

AESCHYLUS · II *FOUR TRAGEDIES*

The Suppliant Maidens. *S. G. Benardete*
The Persians. *S. G. Benardete*
Seven against Thebes. *David Grene*
Prometheus Bound. *David Grene*

SOPHOCLES · I *THREE TRAGEDIES*

Translated and with an Introduction by David Grene

Oedipus the King
Oedipus at Colonus
Antigone

SOPHOCLES · II *FOUR TRAGEDIES*

Ajax. *John Moore*
The Women of Trachis. *Michael Jameson*
Electra *and* Philoctetes. *David Grene*

EURIPIDES · I *FOUR TRAGEDIES*

With an Introduction by Richmond Lattimore

Alcestis. *Richmond Lattimore*
The Medea. *Rex Warner*
The Heracleidae. *Ralph Gladstone*
Hippolytus. *David Grene*

EURIPIDES · II *FOUR TRAGEDIES*

The Cyclops *and* Heracles. *William Arrowsmith*
Iphigenia in Tauris. *Witter Bynner. Introduction by Richmond Lattimore*
Helen. *Richmond Lattimore*

EURIPIDES · III *FOUR TRAGEDIES*

Hecuba. *William Arrowsmith*
Andromache. *John Frederick Nims*
The Trojan Women. *Richmond Lattimore*
Ion. *R. F. Willetts*

EURIPIDES · IV *FOUR TRAGEDIES*

Rhesus. *Richmond Lattimore*
The Suppliant Women. *Frank William Jones*
Orestes. *William Arrowsmith*
Iphigenia in Aulis. *Charles R. Walker*

EURIPIDES · V *THREE TRAGEDIES*

Electra. *Emily Townsend Vermeule*
The Phoenician Women. *Elizabeth Wyckoff*
The Bacchae. *William Arrowsmith*